DYNAMICS OF COMPETITIVE STRATEGY

To our children Cassidy and Conor Smith, Kenny and Erik Grimm, and Marlies and Reid Gannon. Developing appropriate responses to their actions has at times been perhaps the greatest challenge we've faced.

K.G.S.
C.M.G.
M.J.G.

DYNAMICS OF COMPETITIVE STRATEGY

Ken G. Smith
Curtis M. Grimm
Martin J. Gannon

SAGE PUBLICATIONS
International Educational and Professional Publisher
Newbury Park London New Delhi

For information address:

SAGE Publications, Inc.
2455 Teller Road
Newbury Park, California 91320

SAGE Publications Ltd.
6 Bonhill Street
London EC2A 4PU
United Kingdom

SAGE Publications India Pvt. Ltd.
M-32 Market
Greater Kailash I
New Delhi 110 048 India

Printed in the United States of America

Library of Congress Cataloging-in-Publication Data

Smith, Ken G.
Dynamics of competitive strategy / Ken G. Smith, Curtis M. Grimm, Martin J. Gannon.
p. cm.
Includes bibliographical references and index.
ISBN 0-8039-4370-9.—ISBN 0-8039-4371-7 (pbk.)
1. Competition. 2. Strategic planning. I. Grim, Curtis M. II. Gannon, Martin J. III. Title.
HD41.S58 1992
658.4′012—dc20 92-19516
CIP

92 93 94 95 10 9 8 7 6 5 4 3 2 1

Sage Production Editor: Judith L. Hunter

Contents

Preface: The Beginning of a Research Agenda, 1984

It was another one of those lunch debates that only academics seem to enjoy. This one was over the definition of business strategy. When we first started these weekly lunchtime meetings to discuss strategic management issues, none of us thought that we would get so mired in seemingly trivial basic definitions; but in retrospect, we realize that challenging such fundamental notions can lead to important insights.

Although these debates were stimulating, consensus was not a usual outcome, perhaps due to the diverse backgrounds of the participants. Curt Grimm, who approached strategy from an industrial organization economics (IO) background, emphasized environmental and structural dimensions. Curt, who often quoted Porter (1980) and the underlying IO research on which

Porter is based, would argue that firms maximize profits by creating barriers to entry and limiting overall rivalry. Marty Gannon, the management theorist in the bunch, thought of strategy in terms of organizational structure. Marty, who frequently referenced Miles and Snow (1978), would contend that strategy is simply the proper organizational arrangement of people, technology, and administration for the environment the organization faces. The late Frank Paine, on the other hand, who had expertise in strategy and organizational theory, thought of strategy as a gestalt alignment of the organization with its environment. Frank's view was in some sense a compromise between the other two, and he favored Miller and Friesen (1978) to support it.

Ken Smith could appreciate the importance of these definitions, but they did not square perfectly with his business experiences. For Ken, strategy is the plan to beat the competition: to win the contract away from a rival, to swiftly capture a new market before others move, to secretly lock customers in with a long-term contract, to match a rival's pricing behavior or secretly lower prices at a rival's expense. In short, strategy for Ken is to be where the competition is not or, ideally, to have no competition.

One commonality that became clear from our debates was that none of us was particularly comfortable with the current definitions of and approaches to studying business strategy. In particular, the academic definitions seemed to be based on what researchers could easily measure, as opposed to what firms actually did—the actual dynamics of competitive strategy. Moreover, the research rarely focused on samples of competing firms in action with one another. More important, exactly how firms actively utilize strategy to build advantages over competitors seemed to be ignored.

After many seemingly endless debates we decided to center our attention on improving the definition of strategy. This was in 1984 and it marked the beginning of the Strategic Management Research Group (SMRG) at the University of Maryland, which is still active today. The SMRG initially included faculty members Frank Paine, Ken G. Smith, Curtis Grimm, Martin Gannon, and, at various times, Ph.D. students David Barry, Ming-Jer Chen, James Guthrie, Harry Sapienza, August Schomberg, Ken A. Smith, and Leith Wain.

The SMRG meetings became more formal as the goal became clearer. An important breakthrough came when Frank Paine suggested that any definition of strategy should include the concept of competitive timing. But exactly how to include competitive timing in a definition of strategy was perplexing. For example, how should timing be integrated into the various definitions of strategy as: "domain navigation"; "gestalt patterns of behavior"; or "the taking of offensive and defensive actions"? Indeed, we realized that most definitions of strategy had already implicitly included timing, but that the focus was on the idealized long term, not on the timing of actions relative to competitors.

However, by putting aside past definitions of strategy and using competitive timing as a central concept, we began to make progress. Conceiving strategy as a series of races against the clock, we could capture the importance of timing relative to competitors. Each race could be contrived as an event with different racers or players, including quick starters, early leaders, fast finishers, slow seconds, and laggards. This metaphor allowed us to recognize that, although the strategy of "fastest to the finish" is important, there are significant prizes for those firms who are second and third as well. Further, racers may decide to go slowly in one event in order to hold back and save energy for quick action in the next. Finally, with this perspective one can acknowledge that often the early leader is not the winner, and sometimes the slow starter is a fast finisher. These ideas were not well captured in the current definitions of strategy.

A second breakthrough was a forceful change in the unit of analysis—away from the organization or year-end financials as a unit of analysis to a more dynamic competitive event or action/reaction unit of analysis. The key point is that the competitive moves of one firm tend to provoke competitive responses by other firms in the industry. Within the context of this action/response unit of analysis, the timing of actions and reactions becomes of crucial concern.

Our first study focused on the issue of competitive timing with a small sample of high-technology firms. For example, when a firm acts or moves first to introduce a new product or to cut prices, how fast do rivals respond? We asked the chief executive officers of each firm to think of a specific competitive action or move by a rival to which their firms had responded. Gathering data on their responses and response times, the research team identified a number of environmental and organizational factors that affected the speed with which a firm reacts. However, the bottom line of the research was the discovery that response timing and response order were related to organizational performance. In particular, fast and early responders outperformed laggards. The results of this initial research were presented to the Strategic Management Society annual meetings in Philadelphia, Pennsylvania, in October 1984. While the group was encouraged by the very positive feedback from the presentation in Philadelphia, publishing this initial research proved to be a major challenge. Reviewers were overwhelmingly positive about the more active definition of strategy and unit of analysis but concerned about the theory and method. For example, a thoughtful consulting editor for the *Academy of Management Journal* wrote: "First, the authors should consider a conceptual, AMR-type article as a foundation. . . . I believe that this is such an important topic that a very interesting, widely cited piece of work would almost certainly emerge. . . . Second, the study should be expanded. . . . A larger set of firms would permit a more comprehensive analysis."

Thus, the challenge before us was to develop stronger theory and devise a suitable large-sample methodology. The SMRG first focused on theory development. The economics literature was a natural starting point. Led by Curt Grimm, the group spent many months reading the game theory literature. This period was extremely insightful, as there were many direct applications of game theory to the competitive interaction or the moves and responses of firms to one another. Nonetheless, game theory proved limited for developing specific hypotheses regarding the timing and order of competitive moves.

We then spent several additional months reading the organizational literature from sociology and organizational theory. An advancement came from the work of Rogers and Shoemaker (1971) and their application of communication theory to explain the diffusion of technological innovations over time. Communication theory was directly applicable to explaining the timing of competitive moves of firms to one another, and the race metaphor. The idea was that each competitive action carries a message which rivals can interpret and to which they can react at various speeds. Most important, communication theory facilitated the development of specific hypotheses regarding timing and order.

A communication-information model of competitive interaction was then developed and presented at the Academy of Management Annual Meetings in Anaheim, California, in 1988. This model, which serves as the foundation for this book and is fully outlined in Chapter 1, has subsequently guided the group's research. The model facilitated the delineation of the subject matter, as represented by the various chapters, as well as the identification of the principal variables described in each chapter for study.

Overcoming the methodological problems was at least as difficult as solving the theoretical problems. First, there had simply not been any large-scale empirical studies on the timing and order of competitive moves. Thus, there was little guidance in the literature. In addition, we decided early on that a large data base of competitive interactions was required if we were to properly test any hypotheses. Finally, given the unreliability of retrospective reporting by managers, it was determined that a more objective archival method was needed.

Thus, the goal was to find a reliable and comprehensive archival source of competitive events. Ming-Jer Chen, a doctoral candidate at the time and now an assistant professor at Columbia University, worked closely with the group in searching for an archival method of identifying competitive actions and responses. The SMRG spent approximately one year examining alternative archival sources.

After much consideration the group decided to employ a structured content analysis of a major industry publication. In short, the method involved an exhaustive reading and coding of every issue of a major industry publication to identify competitive events. The advantages of the method are that: (a) A large sample of events can be identified; (b) the events can be fully validated from alternative sources; and (c) events can be chronologically ordered to portray first movers and laggards within an event, and ordered across time to capture changing industry rivalry. The specific details of the method, which has now been duplicated with different formats in three other industries, are reported in Chapter 3. We have used this archival method in conjunction with other approaches, as we believe triangulation—combining diverse methodologies—is appropriate.

Once we were armed with a strong theory and a significantly improved methodology, the research advanced rapidly, resulting in a number of academic presentations and journal publications. This book is the culmination of 7 years of research on this new unit of analysis and the dynamics of competitive strategy. The goals of book are to: (a) introduce a comprehensive communication-information model that can serve as a resource for driving research in this area; (b) demonstrate the advantages of the action/response unit of analysis and its influence on the definition of strategy in strategy research; (c) describe some novel methodologies for studying actions and reactions and measuring complex variables; and (d) present empirical results regarding these relationships. Our motivation in writing the book is to inspire additional debate and research on this more dynamic unit of analysis. The SMRG at the University of Maryland continues to explore and debate these issues, and we welcome any comments or suggestions that can help us in our long-term effort of understanding the dynamics of competitive strategy.

We have had considerable help in making this book a reality. The Maryland Business School has provided a uniquely supportive setting, and Dean Rudy Lamone always furnished encouragement and institutional support for our research. The faculty and staff of the University of Limerick, where Ken Smith composed an initial draft of the first seven chapters, were most gracious hosts and commented on presentations of this research. The Small Business Center at Howard University financed certain aspects of this research.

The research would not have been possible without the help of a group of highly talented Ph.D. students who worked as part of the SMRG. Ming-Jer Chen, Harry Sapienza, August Schomberg, Greg Young, and Leith Wain each worked on elements of the research at different times. In particular, Ming-Jer Chen's dissertation research on competitive actions, upon which Chapter 4 draws, and the gathering of the airline data base was a major contribution. In addition, Greg Young's research on the computer retailing firms, his construction of the various data bases, and the production of figures for this book are greatly appreciated. Further, Harry Sapienza co-authored Chapter 2, August Schomberg and Greg Young co-authored Chapter 6, and Leith Wain co-authored Chapter 3.

Our colleagues at the University of Maryland, particularly Ed Locke, Hank Sims, Tom Corsi, Lee Preston, Judy Olian, and Steve Carroll, played a central role in the development of our ideas and in reading and commenting on various research papers and presentations. Their friendship and support are greatly appreciated.

Finally, we acknowledge the wisdom and foresight of the late Frank Paine, Professor of Business and Management at the University of Maryland, for providing us with the initial idea of focusing on competitive timing.

1

A Communication-Information Theory of Competitive Interaction

THIS book focuses on the dynamics of competitive strategy or the active, energetic, and primarily purposeful process by which firms interact with one another as they strive for advantage. The dynamics of competitive strategy are captured empirically by spotlighting the specific competitive actions and reactions of firms to one another. An action is defined as a specific competitive move, such as a price cut or a new product introduction, initiated by a firm to defend or improve its relative competitive position (Chen, 1988). Similarly, a reaction is a

AUTHORS' NOTE: Portions of this chapter were adapted from "A Communication Model of Competitive Response Timing" by K. G. Smith and C. Grimm, 1991, *Journal of Management, 17*, pp. 5-23. Copyright 1991 by the Southern Management Association. Adapted by permission.

discernible counteraction, taken by a competing firm with regard to one or more competitors, that is designed to defend or improve its relative position. Together the action by one firm and the associated responses by rivals combine to constitute a competitive event, which is the central unit of analysis in this book. This book reports on more than 250 competitive events drawn from a variety of industry settings; these events are used to test specific action/response hypotheses derived from communication-information theory.

In this chapter we lay the groundwork for this action/response competitive event perspective. The chapter begins with two case studies and a review of the literature on the action/response unit of analysis. We then highlight the strengths and weaknesses of alternative theories of strategy and competition. In particular, the action/response perspective is compared to macro and micro theories of strategy. Finally, the communication-information model, which serves as a framework for the book, is introduced.

The Competitive Event Perspective

The two case studies in this section are designed to illuminate the competitive event perspective: One represents success and the other failure. We then describe the action/response unit of analysis.

Two Case Studies [1]

The management of Vintech Inc., a division of a large *Fortune* 500 conglomerate, was in turmoil over recent sales declines and the implications of these declines for long-term profits. Corporate management had recently raised the profit goals of this division to make them consistent with its leadership position as an innovator in the sophisticated electronic testing market. Vintech's management, composed primarily of engineers, was now shocked to discover that the division's present sales decline could be attributed to a significant price cut made by its major competitor more than 10 months ago. This competitor, Wellguard, had drastically cut prices in an attempt to increase market share. Vintech's management was now concerned as to the manner in which it should respond. After much deliberation, Vintech's management decided to introduce a new, sophisticated line of products on which it had been working for the past 5 years. Unfortunately for Vintech, there was a considerable delay in getting this line of products to the market. Even though the new product exhibited superior performance capabilities, Vintech's management found it extremely difficult to win back its customers when implementing its response almost 2 years after Wellguard's initial move.

Precision Science's story is very different. Precision Science is a major producer of radar for small aircraft, ships, and military equipment. The company is managed by marketing executives, and the major goal is sales growth. Managers of Precision were somewhat surprised to read press announcements that a major competitor, Mathon, was planning to introduce a new radar product. Management of Precision quickly investigated the performance capabilities of this new product and, within one month after discovering the move, severely cut its prices on competitive products substantially below Mathon's suggested price. This response effectively preempted Mathon's new product move.

The lesson from these two case examples is quite clear: Firms are not independent in the marketplace, but are affected by the actions of one another and are prone to react. Given this interdependence, the effectiveness of a firm's strategy cannot be assessed without an evaluation of the reactions or potential reactions of rivals. For example, an action without a competitive response will generally lead to an advantage for the acting firm. However, an inappropriate action or response, in general, will lead to an advantage for the rival firm. For instance, Vintech responded to Wellguard's major price cuts with a new product introduction. This new product required an extensive marketing campaign with a complete re-education of customers, and resulted in a loss of profits and market share.

Sometimes the key to competitive advantage is not the appropriateness of action but rather its timing or the speed with which a firm acts or reacts. Generally, a longer response time by a rival will result in a competitive advantage for the firm that makes the initial move, and in lower profits for the late responding firm. Precision Science was quite effective in blocking the actions of Mathon by quickly responding with a price cut. Conversely, Vintech was late in responding and suffered disastrous consequences vis-à-vis Wellguard. Moreover, there are occasions in which an acting firm's move can go undetected by rivals for long periods of time, thus providing significant potential monopolistic advantage to the actor, as in the case of Wellguard and Vintech. Alternatively, rivals may fail to respond because they view the actions to be too radical and therefore doomed to fail, thus providing a window of opportunity for the actor to exploit.

The Action/Response Unit of Analysis

As the above discussion suggests, the manner in which a firm acts and reacts with regard to rivals determines in large part the degree to which it will be successful in the marketplace. Figure 1.1 outlines this basic relationship. In short, actions can provoke competitive responses, which combine to form a competitive event. It is argued that the extent of each rival's advantage and profitability is determined by the dynamics involved in these competitive events.

The antecedents for this action/response perspective can be found in the writings of Schumpeter (1934, 1950) and, more recently, Nelson and Winter (1982). According to Schumpeter (1950), some firms intentionally attempt to be industry leaders while others follow and imitate. Both the actions of leaders and the responses by followers are essential to Schumpeter's theory; he viewed the marketplace as a mechanism through which firms experimented by taking specific actions, referred to as

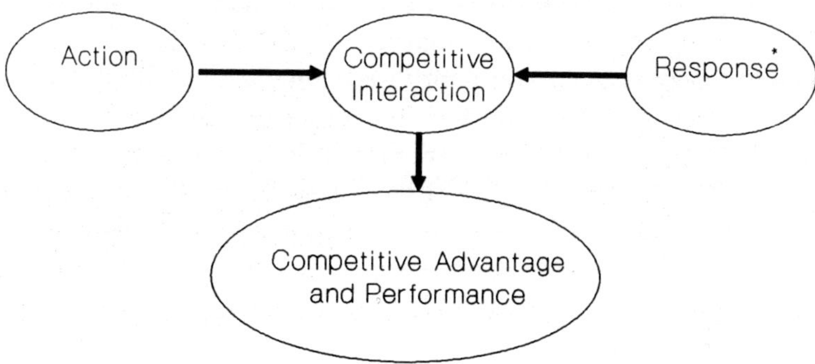

Figure 1.1. The Basic Elements of the Model

innovations. Firms that were successful in carrying out these moves or seizing opportunities reaped profits through the monopolistic position awarded to them by the imitator's lag (Nelson & Winter, 1982). Thus, the firm that was successful in taking actions—clearly, not all firms are successful—whittled away the market from those that did not respond. However, no permanent equilibrium was ever to be reached. The visible profits of the acting firm and the losses experienced by the non-responder motivate the latter to respond and imitate the action.

This action/reaction unit of analysis has been the focal point of numerous game theory models in economics, particularly those models in extensive form. The following example illustrates a game in extensive form where the payoff to the acting firm depends on the rival's reaction. As can be observed in Figure 1.2, when a firm (A) initiates an action, its competitor (R) may have two options in reacting: It can decide either to respond or not to respond. The empirical focus of this book is on those competitive actions that provoke responses. This emphasis is indicated by the dark line running from action through response in the figure.

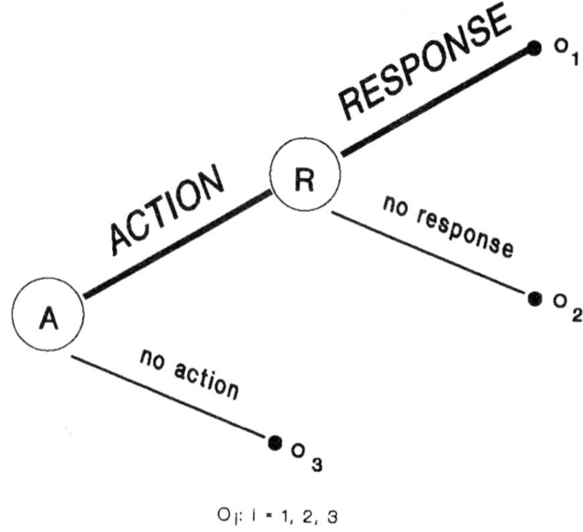

Figure 1.2. A Framework of Competitive Action and Response

A small but significant group of researchers has begun to study the manner by which firms act and react in the marketplace (Chen, 1988; MacMillan, 1983; I. C. MacMillan, 1988; MacMillan, McCaffrey, & Van Wijk, 1985; Nelson & Winter, 1982; Porter, 1980, 1985). In theory, acting firms gain advantage by undertaking actions to which competitors cannot or do not respond. This is the principal assumption behind the barriers to entry literature, as described by Porter (1980, 1985). The firm acting first can earn above-average positive returns from its monopolistic position prior to a rival's response (Lieberman & Montgomery, 1988; Nelson & Winter, 1982). However, any action that generates above-normal profits will lead to a competitive response at some point in time (Schumpeter, 1934, 1950). Therefore, the timing of actions and the designing of such actions so as to maximize the lag in competitors' reactions are crucial elements of this perspective. MacMillan (1988), for example, asserts: "Once the initiative is taken, there is a period when that firm has effective strategic control of the industry, while competitors marshall their resources for the counterattack, and counterattack" (p. 112). Porter (1980) similarly notes: "Other things being equal, the firm wants to make the move that gives it the most time before its competitors can effectively retaliate. . . . Finding strategic moves that will benefit from a lag in retaliation, or making moves so as to maximize the lag, are key principles of competitive interaction" (pp. 95, 98). In addition to the monopolistic position awarded to the first-mover, an extended response lag would allow the acting firm to build experience and other barriers to response, which will translate into a tangible cost or differentiation advantage in the marketplace.

For example, as discussed more fully in Chapter 4, one determinant of the lag in response is the type of move. This can also be modeled with a game in extensive form, as illustrated in Figure 1.3. Assume that there are two moves the acting firm might choose: A_1 is an easy-to-imitate move, such as a price cut, while A_2 is a more difficult-to-imitate move, for example a new product introduction. The responding firm can choose R_1 (a quick response) or R_2 (a slow response). Given A_1, there exists a probability p that the responder chooses R_1, with probability $(1-p)$ that it chooses R_2. Given A_2, there exists a probability q that the responder chooses R_1 and $(1-q)$ that it chooses R_2. One can hypothesize that easy-to-imitate moves will be responded to faster than difficult-to-imitate moves, thus $p>q$.

While acting firms can gain an advantage by executing actions associated with a long response lag, the opposite perspective applies to the responding firm. If a firm judges that a rival's action will lead to above-normal profits, then a response may be necessary. Moreover, as the acting firm is interested in delaying response, a swift response may be imperative to improving the competitive position of the responding firm. For example, a speedy response may allow the responding firm to participate in a quasi-monopoly along with the actor. Baldwin and Childs (1969) label this type of speedy response a "fast-second" strategy. Essentially, by briefly waiting, the "fast-second" firm avoids the risks of acting first, but can nonetheless enjoy

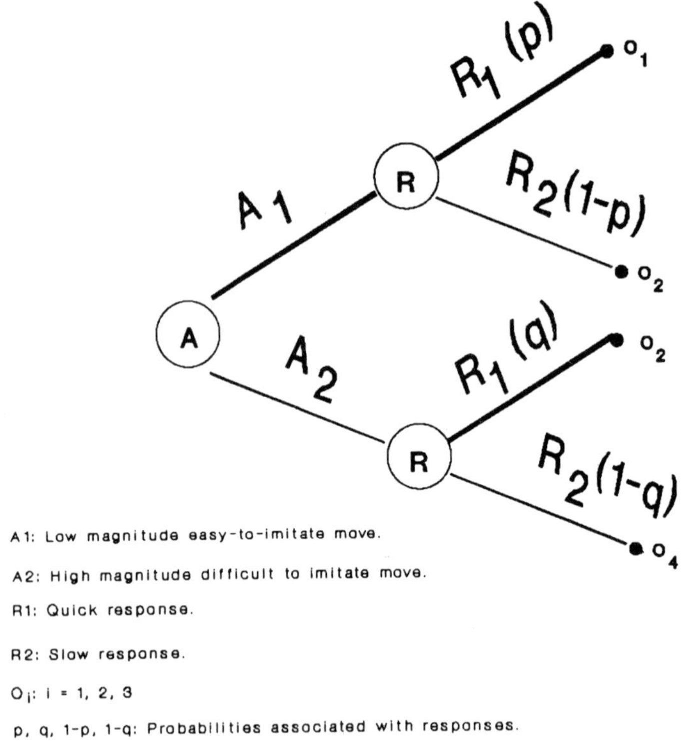

Figure 1.3. A Framework for Predicting Response Lag

the benefits of a positive market reaction by sharing the market with only one competitor, the actor (Lieberman & Montgomery, 1988).

Thus, the principal advantage of the action/response unit of analysis is that it captures the dynamic interaction of competitors as they strive for advantage. More important, the action/response unit of analysis underscores several new dynamic variables for analysis. For example, firms should take actions against competitors having a low probability of acting or responding, that is, a low action or response likelihood, or against firms that respond very slowly, that is, a long response lag.

Another characteristic is response order, or the order in which a firm responds among a group of responders. For example, a firm might take a significant amount of time to respond (increased lag) but still be the first responder among many. Relatedly, actions should be designed to provoke few rather than many rival responses. Of course, there are numerous ways in which firms can respond, but a key response characteristic is imitation or the degree to which the response duplicates the action.

In short, the action/response unit of analysis outlined in Figure 1.1 is the focal point in the dynamic process by which firms build advantage. In the next section of this chapter alternative theories and models of strategy are reviewed relative to this more dynamic action/response perspective.

Macro and Micro Models of Competitive Strategy

Although it is well recognized in the literature that firms are collectively dependent upon one another for success (e.g., Porter, 1980; Scherer & Ross, 1990), researchers have had a difficult time capturing this interdependence in their theories and empirical research. In 1979 Herbert Simon described the current state of knowledge on competition as extremely poor, and he felt that it represented the most poorly researched issue in the field of management. Joskow (1975) summarized the state of empirical knowledge on competition as a "smorgasbord of formal models, ad hoc models, case study information, stories and vague notions." More recently, Caves (1984) appealed for research specifically focusing on "rivalrous moves among incumbent producers."

Alternative theories of competitive strategy can be categorized as either macro or micro. Macro theories and methods tend to be coarse-grained and aimed at understanding general tendencies in strategy, for instance, strategy groups or typologies. In contrast, micro theories and methods are more fine-grained and target more specific strategy phenomena, such as pricing behavior.

Macro Strategy Models

Strategic management researchers have primarily utilized macro approaches to empirically study strategy and competitive advantage (Bettis & Weeks, 1987; Oliva, Day, & MacMillan, 1988). Two macro streams of research, approaching strategy from different theoretical perspectives, are evident in the literature.

The first approach, labeled the "strategic choice perspective," has emphasized the search for the most profitable strategy. For example, strategy researchers have identified a number of different typologies or taxonomies of strategies available to managers and have linked these different strategies to performance (e.g., Buzzell, Gale, & Sultan, 1975; Dess & Davis, 1984; Hatten, Schendel, & Cooper, 1978; Miles & Snow, 1978; Miller & Friesen, 1978; Mintzberg, 1973; Porter, 1980; Wissema, Van der Pol, & Messer, 1980). Researchers utilizing this theoretical perspective typically define strategy as a gestalt pattern of behavior (Hatten et al.) or a pattern in a stream of decisions (Mintzberg) and employ cross-sectional primary or secondary data to identify strategy in a post hoc manner. The well-known Miles and Snow typology of strategy is typical in this stream of research.

Miles and Snow identified four types of strategy from which managers could choose: prospectors, defenders, analyzers, and reactors. Of the four strategies, the reactor strategy, which was merely a reaction to the actions of other firms, resulted in the poorest performance. The remaining three were roughly equal in performance. Similar empirical efforts at the identification of different strategies have been put forth by Miller and Friesen, Hambrick (1983), and Dess and Davis. The practical implications of such research is that firms can build competitive advantage by carefully selecting their distinctive strategies.

Researchers have also studied competitive strategy and advantage by applying theories that link industry structure to the performance of firms within the industry (Bain, 1956; Mason, 1939; Spence, 1977). This macro perspective, labeled the "structural perspective," is best illustrated by the work of Porter (1980). Drawing from decades of literature in industrial organization that commonly analyzes an entire industry rather than a specific firm, Porter formulated a widely accepted structural theory that profits depend on five industry structural forces: entry barriers, substitutes, supplier power, buyer power, and rivalry among competitors. Utilizing year-end financial data and industry structure data in a wide range of studies, strategy researchers have demonstrated the importance of these structural factors for the explanation of profitability (Caves & Porter, 1977; Harrigan, 1980, 1982, 1985; Porter, 1980; Yip, 1982). From such findings it has been asserted that firms can build advantage by being cognizant of and manipulating industry structure.

While these two macro approaches to studying strategy have substantially contributed to strategic management knowledge, especially in providing a general understanding of strategy and the role of industry structure, they face a number of important limitations. One important weakness of most of the strategy/performance research rests on the assumption that broad patterns of strategy behavior portray a firm's actual competitive behavior in the marketplace. For instance, the assumption is that Miles and Snow's prospector strategy (a firm that emphasizes innovation), derived from year-end financial data (e.g., R&D expenditures), is reflective of how this firm behaves vis-à-vis its competitors. Unfortunately, there is no evidence that strategic gestalts or broad patterns of strategic behavior, especially derived from annual financial data, are reflective of firms' actual competitive behavior on a day-to-day basis. In fact, the prospector may be a frequent innovator but also a major price cutter relative to its competition.[2]

Tests of industrial economic structural theories face similar difficulties. For example, structural forces such as entry barriers and rivalry must often be inferred from indicators available only in annual financial statements, such as the amount of fixed assets. Unfortunately, there have been few efforts to link financial information to actual entry or exit behavior. Similarly, the level of competition or rivalry in an industry has often been inferred from the number of competitors or the concentration ratio without actually gathering data on rivalry.

Thus, a major criticism of both approaches is the failure to measure the dynamics of actual strategic behavior or strategic conduct. Instead, researchers must rely on indirect indicators in order to make inferences about strategy or firm conduct. In summary, researchers employing these two macro perspectives may never be able to glean the fine details of competitive interaction and advantage. Bettis and Weeks (1987) note that macro models "cannot be used to study the micro competitive dynamism of an industry" (p. 550), while Oliva, Day, and MacMillan (1988) emphasize that macro models are "incapable of handling the diversity of behavior required to describe the full range of competitive processes" (p. 374). However, a more dynamic and fine-grained approach has been suggested in the literature on microeconomics.

Microeconomic Models

Microeconomic models have long held promise for strategy researchers because they are designed to model strategic competitive interaction. Although such models have been used to mathematically denote equilibrium outcomes and payoffs associated with alternative actions and responses, they have rarely been used in empirical strategy research (Bettis and Weeks, 1987, is one exception).

Micro models in economics have tended to emphasize price competition, since this is fundamental to the oligopoly problem. For the monopolistic and perfectly competitive cases, such models provide a rich theoretical structure. However, Chamberlain (1957) argued that the competition between two firms may lead to a determinant price anywhere between the monopoly price and the perfectly competitive price, depending on the behavioral assumptions. Unfortunately, specifying the behavioral assumptions proves to be exceedingly difficult. Baumol (1972) proposed two important assumptions: (a) to ignore firm interdependence; or (b) to assume that each competitor is a rational economic agent and deduce behavior by determining the set of actions and responses that maximize each firm's expected utility. These two assumptions are fundamental to the two most important microeconomic models of strategy and competition: reaction function models and game theory (Von Neumann & Morgenstern, 1944).

The original reaction function model was proposed by Cournot, in 1838. The Cournot hypothesis is that when firms attempt to select the ideal strategy or action to pursue, each firm can assume the rival firm's output to be constant. Since the rival's output level is not responsive (does not react) to the actor's own output, the firm can determine the most appropriate profit-maximizing strategic action. However, assuming equal capabilities among competitors means that these rivals may see profit opportunities simultaneously and adjust their output accordingly within their reaction curves. When two or more firms seek opportunities by adjusting their output (a very likely case), the model leads to unpredictable results. Although many have tried to resolve this problem, Simon (1980) has declared that observed reactions in the marketplace are generally far too complex to be captured by such a simple model.

In recent years there has been great interest in game theory as a vehicle for modeling strategic competitive behavior (Bettis & Weeks, 1987; Karnani & Wernerfelt, 1985; Weigelt & MacMillan, 1988). Game theory's usefulness in a competitive setting lies in its applicability to modeling and predicting the payoffs to various strategic alternatives in competitive situations involving actions and reactions. Kreps (1990), a leading game theorist, points out that achieving an equilibrium solution generally requires strong assumptions about player's objectives and tendencies, whereas players can quite naturally take a very different course of behavior, which would not lead to an equilibrium. Also, there are strong assumptions regarding information availability in game theory models. For example, a major limitation of Weigelt and MacMillan's work on the interactive strategic analysis framework is the assumption that "certain parameters [of the model] are common knowledge [to the players], especially the subjective probability distributions" (p. 37). In addition, Rapoport (1966) has shown that the common assumption that each competitor is a rational economic actor leads to paradoxical results, and that these equivocal results impede game theory's usefulness as a prescriptive tool for most strategy problems.

Another limitation of game theory is the precise, exact, and somewhat simplified specification as to strategies available to managers. Kreps (1990) notes that real-life competitive interaction is too rich and full of possible combinations of moves and countermoves to be modeled by game theory. As an example, he cites the recently deregulated U.S. domestic air-transport business, one industry from which the current sample is drawn:

> In this fairly complex situation, players (rival firms) were unclear on what others would do, how they would behave, and what were their motivations. Each individual firm could try to make assessments of what others would do and choose accordingly optimal responses, but it would have been rather a surprise if the behaviour so engendered the equilibrium of any game-theoretic model that didn't begin with that behavior and then construct the model around it. (p. 138)

As these arguments suggest, classical reaction functions and game theory are of limited value for representing real competitive behavior. Indeed, the levels of abstraction and strict assumptions required for deriving clear-cut equilibrium outcomes in economics are generally inappropriate for the more applied task of the strategic management research. More important, both models ignore the processes by which firms arrive at different action/response decisions. Communication-information theory avoids these problems, as suggested in the next section of this chapter.

Communication-Information Theory and the Action/Response Perspective

Chester Barnard (1938) noted that: "In an exhaustive theory of organization, communication would occupy a central place,

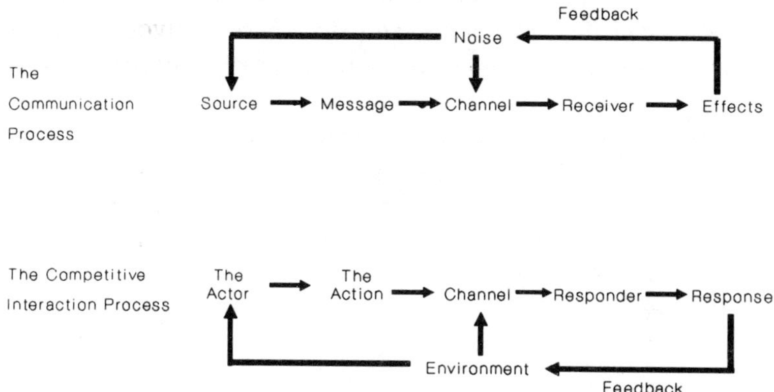

Figure 1.4. The Communication Process and the Competitive Interaction Process Are Similar

because the structure, extensiveness, and scope of the organization are almost entirely determined by communication techniques" (p. 91). The conceptual origins of organizational communication theory were initially provided by Barnard (1938) and Thompson (1967), but the theory has subsequently been more thoroughly developed by Miller (1972), Simon (1973), Galbraith (1973, 1977), Tushman and Nadler (1978), and Huber (1982). Theories of organizational communication have been utilized to explain a wide variety of organizational phenomena, ranging from strategy and structure (Egelhoff, 1982; Galbraith, 1973) to decision making (Duncan, 1973; Van de Ven, Delbecq, & Koenig, 1976) and innovation adoption rates (Rogers 1983). For a complete review, the reader is referred to McPhee and Tompkin (1985) or Jablin, Putnam, Roberts, and Porter (1987).

The basic stimulus/response model of communication, initially suggested by Shannon and Weaver (1949) and refined by Berlo (1960), is outlined in the top of Figure 1.4. The model consists of a source transmitting a message over a channel to a receiver. Noise, or competing stimuli, can be present with the message in the channel (Mortensen, 1972). From a process point of view, the acts of one element (the stimulus) have the effect of creating changes in another element (the response), which in turn can feed back to effect changes in others, including the initial communicator.

Communication-information theory can furnish a very useful underpinning for studying and explaining competitive actions and responses. First, communication theory provides direct insight into the fundamental and key components of a model of competition. As can be seen in Figure 1.4, the communicator in the model parallels the competitor who undertakes an action; the message facet is similar to the competitive action that is undertaken; and the receiver is equivalent to the rival, who may or may not respond. Messages, just as competitive actions, are communicated through channels while noise or the environment can influence the process. Responses then feed back to trigger new actions or additional responses by other competitors. Therefore, communication theory provides direct insight into the salient dimensions relevant to a dynamic model of competitive interaction and competitive advantage.

Second, communication theory allows for a more focused orientation to the process of competition. This process orientation, as opposed to the traditional content orientation of macro and micro models, should provide a deeper and improved understanding of how and why firms compete. For example, the application of communication theory can provide insight into the dynamic, multivariate and time-ordered process in which many factors interact to influence the action or response decision.

Third, communication theory emphasizes information and how this information flows (Fisher, 1978). Indeed, it is well recognized in the communication literature that information spreads irregularly through a system, arriving at different locations at different times (Guetzkow, 1965). The fact that information arrives at different locations at different points of time has been an important aspect of communication research. For example, communication theory researchers have identified a number of concepts, such as opinion leadership (Rogers, 1983), homophily or the similarity of the communicators (Lazarsfeld & Merton, 1964), message content (Berlo, 1960), noise (Shannon & Weaver, 1949), and information processing characteristics (Knight & McDaniel, 1979) that help to explain the timing, quality, and flow of information in a system.

Information is also a critical component of interfirm rivalry. Porter (1980) describes this aspect of rivalry:

> The behavior of competitors provides signals in a myriad of ways. Some signals are bluffs, some are warnings, and some are earnest commitments to a course of action. Market signals are indirect means of communicating in the marketplace, and most if not all of a competitor's behavior can carry *information* that can aid in competitor analysis and strategy formulation. (p. 75, emphasis added)

In short, in the highly uncertain competitive setting, a competitor's action carries information, expressed or implied, that firms must evaluate and process to successfully compete. Thus, well-researched communication concepts can be applied to explain the timing, quality, and flow of competitive information among a set of competitors.

Finally, communication theory clearly fits the dynamic action/response unit of analysis of this book and is therefore more appropriate than alternative theories or models. In fact, the model proposed in this book explicitly captures both the actions of firms as they attempt to carry out their strategy to gain a competitive advantage and the responses of competitors as they strive for potentially incompatible positions.

Consequently, the model has the potential to be more dynamic and fine-grained than macro strategy models. Nonetheless, the model is also quite consistent with the goals and objectives of traditional macro strategy models. For example, by focusing on a firm's actions or responses, one can directly assess the firm's strategy. For example, one could conclude that a firm that primarily engages in price-cutting actions is attempting to carry out a "build" market share strategy emphasizing lower costs. This approach may prove to be an important benefit when compared to the conventional aggregated coarse-grained approaches, in that the firm's actions are clearly reflective of its intentions. Consequently, the action/reaction approach is proactive, as the operationalization of strategy should be. Moreover, one can directly assess the effectiveness of various mobility/entry barriers to deter a response. In this regard, the researcher could study actions designed to raise barriers to entry, such as capacity expansion, and then specifically investigate whether a response (in this case, entry) occurred. Such a method would provide a more fine-grained alternative to inferring, from static correlations, that barriers are effective in limiting entry or mobility. The focus on competitive rivalry is also consistent with industry structural models in that actions and response can have an important impact on the current and future structure of an industry (Porter, 1980).

Further, the model offers significant advantages over alternative microeconomic models of strategy. In particular, communication theory deals with forms of bounded rationality that are not well accommodated by game theories, and the model does not make assumptions about the output levels of rivals. Most important, the model allows for the modeling of processes of the firm that are generally too complex for the current state of microeconomic analysis.

This discussion demonstrates the significance of communication theory in providing insight into the nature of actions and responses. Communication-information concepts will be utilized throughout this book to develop and test hypotheses regarding the determinants of competitive actions and response. In particular, information and the manner in which it flows, will serve as an underpinning for each of the hypotheses.[3]

The Communication-Information Model

Figure 1.5 identifies the basic components of the model as derived from communication theory. The components of the model include: the actor or the firm that takes a competitive

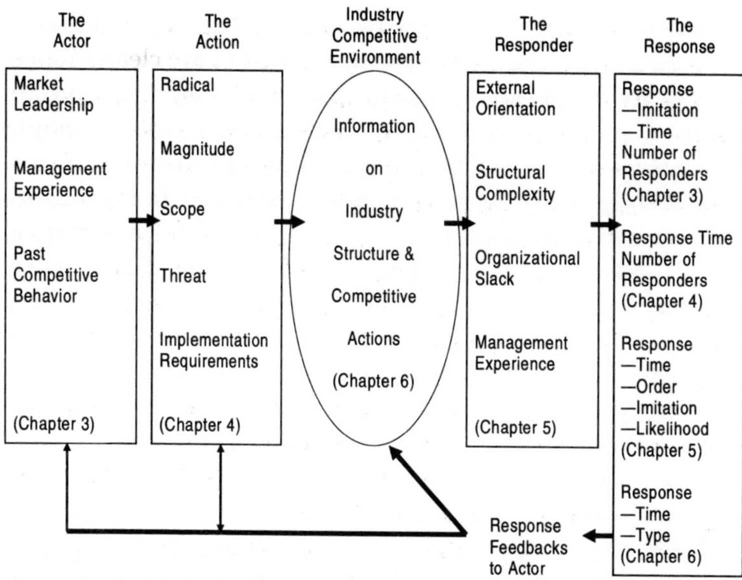

Figure 1.5. A Model of Competitive Interaction

action; the action itself, which may be a new product introduction, a price cut, a new advertising campaign, and so forth; the potential responder, assumed to be a competitor; a communication channel connecting actor and responder, which could be a common supplier, common customer, or public reports of the action; and noise in the environment, which can influence the manner in which the responding firm decodes the competitor's action. A feedback loop is included to signify that a response can act as a new stimulus evoking other responses.

Actions and responses are explained in the model from the perspective of the decision-making process of the firms involved. This decision process is conceived as an information-seeking and information-processing activity in which the firm is motivated to reduce uncertainty about the potential advantages and disadvantages of a market opportunity or threat (Huber & Daft, 1987). For the actor, the process begins with the search for a market opportunity or an opportunity to improve the firm's current competitive position. For the responding firm, the process begins when that firm is first exposed to information on a rival's action—the stimulus (Berlo, 1960). This action creates uncertainty for rivals, which in turn leads to greater information processing (Galbraith, 1977).

It is now possible to describe the chapters of the book in terms of the model. Chapter 2 discusses alternative methodologies for studying actions and responses. The chapter outlines the research methods employed in this book as well as the principal variables under study. As noted, some of the key variables of interest include the alternative types of actions and responses that firms can undertake, the timing of responses, the rank order in which competitors respond, the likelihood of response, and the degree to which responses imitate actions.

Chapter 3 focuses on the firm that acts first or makes the initial move. Hypotheses are presented regarding the important role of reputation in rivalry. More specifically, we use reputation characteristics of the actor to predict response. The basic argument is that firms undertaking actions vary in terms of reputations and commitment in the marketplace (Huber & Daft, 1987; Porter, 1980); as a result, rivals will use the reputation of the actor as information in making response decisions.

Chapter 4 analyzes the nature of actions that firms undertake and the manner in which these actions can be used to predict response. While the physical product of interpersonal communication is the message, the physical product of competition can be the action. From a communication perspective, an action, like an interpersonal message, can provide important signals to rivals. Several important information characteristics of actions are identified in this chapter, and they include the magnitude of the action, the scope of the action, the threat of the action, and the implementation requirements of the action. These characteristics are used to predict response characteristics.

Chapter 5 spotlights the characteristics of the responding firm. From a communication perspective, responders must perceive and process information on a rival's actions in order to make a response decision. The manner in which firms decode information on competitors and their actions depends on their information-processing systems and capacities (Huber & Daft, 1987; March & Simon, 1958). Information flows throughout the organization are used to explain the decision of how to respond (Knight & McDaniel, 1979; Mortensen, 1972). Specific hypotheses concerning information sensory systems, information analyzing mechanisms, and information selection and retention are used in this chapter to predict characteristics of response.

Chapter 6 emphasizes the important role of the competitive environment in strategy and competitive advantage. The various moves that firms undertake with regard to one another represent an important part of an industry's structure or competitive environment (Porter, 1980). From a communication perspective, this environment can be conceived in terms of the amount and variety of information on industry actions, the actors, and the channels through which this information must pass. Accordingly, as the number of competitive actions increases in an industry, so too do the amount and spectrum of information available to decision makers. The chapter also serves to integrate findings from previous chapters by considering the specific industry context in which actions and responses are carried out.

Chapter 7 examines the performance consequences of acting and responding, in particular, the performance consequences of move order and timing in rivalry. Chapter 8 presents an alternative view to out-competing one's rivals: namely, how firms can collectively benefit from minimizing rivalry. And Chapter 9 summarizes and integrates the general results of the book.

As in any research study, we have made certain assumptions about the subject at hand. First, it is clear that not all competitive actions prompt the responses of rivals. Nonetheless, for the sample of events under consideration, we must assume that a firm's action provides either an opportunity or a threat to rival firms, thus motivating them to respond. We make this assumption since the research considers only situations in which actions provoke responses.

Second, when a firm undertakes an action or a response, we assume that it rarely knows a priori what the outcome of this move will be. Indeed, a central tenet of our theory is that the successfulness of actions and responses often depends on complex combinations of factors, including the reputation of the actor and the action undertaken; the environment in which the action and responses occur; and the timing, number, and nature of the rivals' responses. Given this complexity, we assume that the outcomes of competitive actions and responses are virtually always uncertain to managers at the onset.

Finally, although we readily acknowledge that much competitive interaction involves bluffing, signaling, and deception between rivals, these facets of competition are largely beyond the bounds of the current research. That is, the current research examines only settings in which actions evoke reactions, without focusing in detail on the managerial intentions behind these actions.

Notes

1. The names of these companies are fictitious.

2. A related limitation of much of this research pertains to the samples employed. Much of strategy and performance research has not controlled for a potential competitor's strategic behavior. For example, the typical samples under consideration generally have not been so exhaustive as to include all of a firm's competitors in the sample. Thus, strategies that lead to high performance may in fact be ineffective when considered in light of competitors' strategies that were not included for study.

3. One exception is Chapter 8, where game theory is used to highlight the value of cooperative strategies.

2

A Methodology for Studying Competitive Actions and Responses

THIS chapter focuses on alternative methodologies for studying the actions and responses of rivals to one another, and then lays out in some detail the methodologies to be employed in this book. We begin with a brief review and critique of the current approaches or methodologies for studying the dynamics of strategy. Not surprisingly, these approaches are related to the alternative theoretical perspectives discussed in the previous chapter. For example, macro strategy theories have generally

---

AUTHORS' NOTE: Portions of this chapter were adapted from "Selecting Methodologies for Entrepreneurial Research: Trade-Offs and Guidelines" by K. G. Smith, M. J. Gannon, and H. J. Sapienza, 1989, *Entrepreneurship: Theory and Practice, 14*, pp. 39-49.

been tested through very coarse-grained, cross-sectional approaches utilizing secondary methodologies, whereas micro theorists have generally used case studies based on primary methods or first-hand observations. Because this book is devoted to the dynamics of competitive actions and responses, it concentrates on the presentation of empirical evidence, not upon method per se. However, very little attention has been devoted to the methods of studying the dynamics of strategy, and since this book will employ a number of innovative approaches, a review of alternative procedures is appropriate and necessary to properly introduce the methodology employed in this book.

First, we discuss the strengths and weaknesses of alternative approaches of studying actions and responses by considering the trade-offs researchers must face in the selection of methods. A central argument is that each method has certain strengths and weaknesses, and that the optimal research approach should employ multiple methods or triangulation (Denzin, 1978; Jick, 1979). Accordingly, the actions and responses reported in this book were identified through a combination of primary methods (case studies, expert panels, surveys, and interviews) and secondary methods (major industry publications and corporate records). Second, we introduce and describe in detail the various methodologies employed in this book. Finally, we present and define the key dynamic variables emphasized in this book.

Alternative Methods: Trade-Offs

The dynamics of strategy can be studied using primary methods (often considered subjective techniques) involving investigator, management, and outsider inference, or more observer independent secondary methods (considered objective techniques). These different techniques can be arranged on a continuum extending from the more objective to the more subjective. Examples of action and response data derived from secondary methods include a firm's pricing behavior, as obtained from archival corporate records or financial statements; all new product developments during a given year, as obtained from an organization's promotional literature, R&D records, and patent filings; and competitive events, as reported in industry-specific news media or major press publications. Examples of action and response data derived from more primary methods include the identification of actions and responses by managers provided in questionnaires and interviews and/or the ratings of actions and responses by external experts, such as industry consultants.

We can consider the various issues involved in the selection of a method to study actions and responses by focusing on the strengths and weaknesses associated with whether the method employed is primary or secondary. Of principal concern is the relationship between these different methods and vital issues pertaining to the validity and reliability of action and response measures. Also of concern are questions of the research objective, research timing, and research efficiency. Although each of these topics is discussed separately, it is recognized that many of these concerns are interrelated.

Valid and Reliable Measures

It is possible to evaluate the question of obtaining valid and reliable measures of actions and responses by focusing on issues of research specificity, construct validity, data biases, and flexibility. At this point it is important to repeat our basic definition of a competitive event: the specific action of one firm and the responses to it by other firms. An event is a specific occurrence or milepost that can occur at any time during a given period, for example, an action and/or response can occur on January 1, or May 3, or at any point in a given time period. Many times the strategy researcher employing secondary methods is limited in the specificity of the unit of analysis or competitive event that can be studied because the objective data are aggregated; for example, financial statements reflect a year's activity. Research employing secondary methods has been appropriately labeled coarse-grained because the specific details are masked by the aggregation of data being used (Harrigan, 1983). For example, year-end financial data do not allow one to assess the number of price cuts a firm made in a given year. Primary techniques, because they more often can be constructed around a particular event (action and response), offer greater precision; they can be precisely targeted to the event and therefore have been referred to as fine-grained (Harrigan, 1983).

Related to the issue of event specificity is that of construct validity. Frequently researchers using secondary techniques must accept loose and incomplete operational definitions of the constructs they are attempting to measure. For example, a researcher might use average unit price (total revenue divided by number of units sold) to reflect a firm's pricing strategy. A low average price might suggest a price-cutting strategy vis-à-vis competitors. But these data may not reflect the firm's actual strategic behavior. That is, the firm may have the lowest average price but may not have engaged in any price-cutting activity. A firm with a higher average price may have experienced wide variation in pricing behavior and may have actually cut prices during the preceding period. Poor correspondence between operational definition and target concept undermines construct validity and can mask important micro strategic behaviors. In contrast, the researcher enjoys more flexibility with a primary method in that the study can be specifically designed around the particular event. Such flexibility is especially useful in the study of actions and responses, because often the causal effects of such interaction are very subtle or small in magnitude. Such flexibility is frequently not possible when the researcher is relying on a secondary method.

The issue of bias is also important. When the only knowledgeable raters who could provide information on actions and responses are likely to contaminate the reporting, secondary methods are preferable. This preference may be especially important in the reporting of rivalrous actions and responses, which can be considered sensitive data. Consequently, managers may intentionally or unintentionally provide inaccurate information. For instance, it is possible that when asked to identify a specific competitive event, the respondent may describe the event as different from the firm's actual behavior, perhaps fearing that revealing the firm's true behavior will provide an advantage to competitors. Also, a respondent responsible for a particular function, such as marketing, is likely to remember a particular event differently from someone who is responsible for another function, for example, finance. Finally, Allison (1971) has demonstrated that researchers bring their own set of biases and constraints to each research study. They may evoke a certain bias in measures of actions and responses just by the manner in which they ask certain questions. Even their presence during an interview can bias responses.

In addition, it is often difficult to employ primary methods because there exist only a few experts inside and outside the firm who have the requisite knowledge. Moreover, these experts may not agree on certain strategic events because of differing degrees of information, different agendas, and so on. Using more objective secondary methods tends to minimize these biases.

The Research Question

Another concern that influences the selection of method is the purpose of the research, or whether the researcher is attempting to study management intentions or behaviors. Mintzberg (1978) distinguished between a firm's intended, emergent, and realized strategy. He noted that management's intentions may not always reach fruition. For example, a new product introduction may fail or may never be fully carried out (e.g., the introduction of New Coke by Coca-Cola). Likewise, he recognized that strategies may evolve and be realized in the absence of intentions. For example, a firm with a record of slow imitation of rivals may overcome rivals who mistakenly introduced a new product with little sales potential. In this instance there may be a benefit to the firm with the emergent (albeit unintended) imitation strategy. Distinguishing between deliberate (intended and realized) and emergent (unintended and realized) strategic actions requires information about strategic intentions. The point is that researchers must decide whether they want to study strategic intentions or behaviors. Clearly, the method selected has major implications for the decision. When a researcher wants to understand intentions of managers in taking an action or response, primary methods are preferable. On the other hand, if the researcher is interested only in studying actual behaviors without regard for intentions, greater reliance can be placed on secondary methods.

Time Span

The timing of the research is also crucial to the method. Given the time-ordered and dynamic nature of actions and responses, much of the research will have to be conducted after the event occurs. Secondary methods are generally preferable to primary methods in such analyses. Frequently, observers of actions and responses will tend to disagree among themselves as to what happened and, even if they do agree, there is always the issue of whether their viewpoint coincides with the actual facts of the situation.[1]

One possible alternative is longitudinal primary field research. Researchers might periodically visit a set of firms to assess their organizational actions and responses over time. While such research is extremely valuable, frequently it cannot be conducted because of cost constraints and/or managerial resistance. Hence, if the study is to cover an extended series of actions and responses over time, the only alternative may be a secondary methodology, and this will be especially true if the researcher desires a large data set amenable to statistical analysis. For example, Bettis and Weeks (1987) employed a secondary method, based on news reporting of the actions and responses of Kodak and Polaroid to one another over a 2-year period, in the instant photography industry, to make inferences about rivalry and performance. Finding reliable primary observers over such a long period of time would have been difficult.

Efficiency

Secondary methods, which rely on data that have already been collected, are frequently easier and cheaper to obtain than primary methods that require fieldwork. Admittedly, survey data may also be economical; however, the return rate on survey research is often poor, and it is frequently difficult to obtain responses from multiple subjects within a firm. The alternative to such a survey is for the researcher to visit each firm to conduct interviews. This alternative can be extremely time-consuming and costly, particularly in dealing with related chains of actions and responses among different rivals who may be geographically dispersed. In contrast, secondary methods relying on preexisting data can often be accessed much more economically since the costs are spread across a large number of researchers and institutions.

A Case for Method Triangulation

As the discussion suggests, there are important trade-offs in the selection of a research method or methods that directly or indirectly concern the validity and reliability of action and response measures. Table 2.1 summarizes these factors, all of which have been discussed. A plus sign indicates that the researcher should favor the use of a particular method; a minus sign indicates the opposite.

Overall, the analysis suggests that *both primary and secondary methods* should be employed in the identification of actions and responses. With multiple methods or triangulation, the research can overcome the potential weaknesses inherent in any one method. The call for multiple methods was initially suggested by Campbell and Fiske (1959), who developed the concept of "multiple operationalism." The logic underlying multiple operationalism is that convergence between two different measures obtained through disparate methods in one study ensures that the variance reflected by the construct is not the result of any one method (referred to as single method variance). Thus

Table 2.1 Factors Influencing Choice of Research Method

	Secondary	*Primary*
Validity and Reliability		
research specificity	–	+
construct validity	–	+
observer bias	+	–
availability	+	–
Research Objective		
strategic intentions	–	+
strategic behaviors	+	–
Time Perspective		
post hoc analysis	+	–
longitudinal studies	+	–
Efficiency		
costs (time, human resources)	–	+
costs (monetary)	–	+

SOURCE: Adapted from "Selecting Methodologies for Entrepreneurial Research: Trade-offs and Guidelines" by K. G. Smith, M. J. Gannon, and H. J. Sapienza, 1989, *Entrepreneurship: Theory and Practice*, *14*(1), pp. 39-49. Adapted by permission.

convergence enhances the likelihood that the results are valid and not a methodological artifact (Bouchard, 1976).

Further, writers such as Denzin (1978) and Jick (1979) have emphasized the importance of triangulation of methods in research. Jick defined triangulation as the "combination of methodologies in the study of the same phenomena" (p. 291). Triangulation offers a number of benefits. As Bouchard observed, convergence of results through triangulation enhances precision; however, triangulation provides more than reliability and validation in that it "captures a more complete, holistic and contextual portrayal of the units under study" (Jick, p. 603).

Research Methods

The research methods described in this book embrace the goal of method triangulation. Indeed, the actions and responses were identified through a combination of primary and secondary

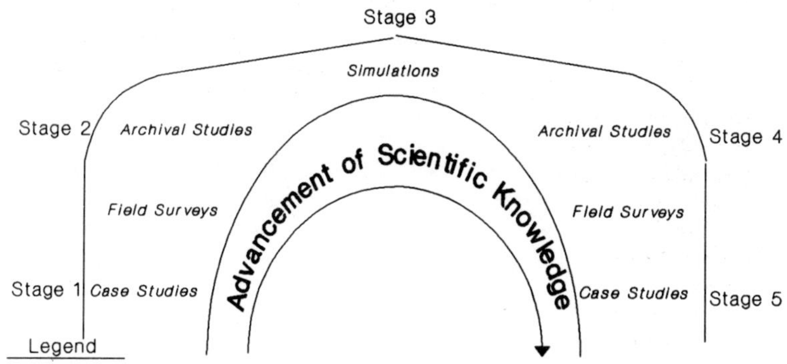

Figure 2.1. Modified Depiction of McGrath's (1964) Horseshoe of the Advancement of Scientific Knowledge.

From "Toward a 'Theory and Method' for Research on Organization" by J. E. McGrath in W. W. Cooper, H. L. Leavitt, and M. W. Shelly, *New Perspectives in Organizatonal Research,* John Wiley, 1964, pp. 533-547. Reprinted with permission of Carnegie Mellon University.

methods. These included primary methods such as case studies, expert panels, surveys, and interviews, as well as secondary methods such as major industry publications and corporate records. By triangulating the various actions and responses, the authors have attempted to overcome the weaknesses inherent in any one method.

While method triangulation is a significant strength of the research reported in this book, it should be recognized that the studies and methods were not all conducted simultaneously. Instead, the approach mirrors McGrath's (1964) horseshoe of the evolution of scientific progress (see Figure 2.1). More specifically, our studies began as simple case studies, moved to more robust primary survey methods and secondary archival methods, and concluded with fine-grained case studies. Thus, the studies built on one another, with each work reflecting a greater understanding on the part of the researchers of the important issues and questions surrounding the dynamics of competitive strategy. In total, four studies were conducted in three separate industries.

Table 2.2 Four Studies in Three Industries

Type of Industry	*Emerging Growth*	*Emerging Growth*	*Mature*	*Fragmented*
Study number	1	2	3	4
	High Tech Electronic	High Tech Electronic	U.S. Domestic Airlines	Computer Retailing
N	22	25	32	27
Method	Case Study	Case Study	Archival Content Analysis	Case Study

Each of the methods was designed to measure the specific actions and responses of rivals to one another. As noted earlier, an *action* was defined as a specific market move, such as a price cut, a market expansion, or a special promotion. A *response* is also a market move, taken by a competing firm to counteract the initial competitive action. All of the methods that will now be discussed are summarized in Table 2.2.

Studies 1 and 2: The Electrical Manufacturing and High Technology Studies

The first two studies involved intensive case study interviews and questionnaire administration with chief executives officers (CEOs) from electrical manufacturing firms and high-technology electronics firms. These two industries were selected because they are emerging growth industries noted for their relatively high degree of competition and a general lack of structural barriers (Porter, 1980). The electrical manufacturing study included 22 firms, while the high technology study involved 25 firms.

The mean sales volume for the two samples was about the same: $27 million, ranging from $275,000 to $500 million (see Exhibit 2.1 for the high-tech firms participating in Study 2). The products of firms in the samples ranged from electric switches to sophisticated computer and space electrical components.

Exhibit 2.1 Characteristics of Sample Firms

Principal Product	*Yearly Sales Volume (in thousands)*	*Number of Employees*
1. Digital-switching systems	15,000*	120*
2. Voice data-entry equipment	5,000	50*
3. Precision light-control devices	11,000	100
4. High-frequency antennas	2,000*	20*
5. Digital signal-processing equipment	22,000*	300
6. Long-distance data-transmission equipment	51,000	750
7. High-speed integrated circuit technology	875,000	2,350
8. Ultraviolet illumination technology	8,000*	50*
9. Digital remote controls	40,000	500
10. Electronic warfare systems	1,500,000	3,000
11. Custom television remote systems	3,000	35
12. Laser light technology	400,000	1,750
13. Frequency multiplexer and bandpass filters	2,000*	85*
14. Integrated work stations	100,000	900
15. Digital multiplex equipment	500,000	5,000
16. Modems, multiplexers, and power conversion equipment	120,000	1,100
17. Frequency synthesizers	1,000	20
18. Printed circuit boards	10,000	400
19. Digital data systems	376,000	2,200*
20. Protocol converters	19,000	125
21. Surveillance and communication equipment	3,500	75
22. Electronic sampling equipment	80,000	500
23. Electronic simulators	500,000*	800*
24. Diagnostic instruments	30,000	370
25. Medical testing systems	15,000*	400*

* Author's estimate

The first step in the data-collection process was extensive interviewing of each firm's executive officers. Through the interviews the researchers were able to identify meaningful ways of measuring actions and responses. That is, the input from executives was important in helping the authors ascertain that the identified actions and responses could be totally verified and that they were deemed important by all of the competitors involved. In addition, the interviews were helpful for gathering background data on each firm and for soliciting the support of each firm for the second phase of the study.

In the second phase a formal questionnaire was developed and administered to the CEOs, who was asked to identify an important *competitive action* in their industry to which their firm responded. These managers were then asked a number of questions regarding not only the nature of the action but also the nature and timing of their response. A number of other relevant background questions were also included in the questionnaire.

Study 3: The U.S. Airline Industry

The method utilized in Study 3 has been labelled "structured content analysis" (Jauch, Osborn, & Martin, 1980). Specifically, a series of important *competitive events* in the U.S. airline industry were identified from an 8-year review of all the issues of *Aviation Daily*; and a predesigned, structured coding schedule was used to perform the content analysis of each event. This methodology has not been previously employed to analyze competitive interaction. Accordingly, specific aspects of the method, including selection of industry, source of action and response data, procedures for identification of actions and responses, and treatment of industry segmentation, will be discussed in some detail.

The U.S. domestic airline industry was selected for study because of its acknowledged competitiveness, well-known set of competitors, clearly defined boundary (single businesses), and rich source of public information. The domestic airline industry is defined as all major airlines with annual operating revenues in excess of $100 million (see Exhibit 2.2 for details of the sample). Important competitive events of the domestic airline industry, including those of 32 major and national airlines

Exhibit 2.2 Sample Airlines With 1986 Level of Output

Airlines	*Revenue Passenger Miles**
AirCal	10,658,299
Air Florida	na
Alaska	2,614,414
Aloha	379,070
America West	3,233,085
American	43,860,797
Braniff	2,541,833
Capitol	na
Continental	17,414,912
Delta	28,970,446
Eastern	31,831,422
Frontier	2,960,661
Hawaiian	2,332,226
Jet America	970,008
Midway	1,947,102
New York Air	1,991,399
Northwest	15,143,864
Ozark	2,262,432
Pan Am	4,572,732
Pacific Southwest	4,293,391
People Express	8,896,270
Piedmont	10,232,273
Republic	9,451,587
Southwest	5,666,038
Texas Air	na
TransAmerica	na
Trans World	17,563,320
United	51,556,931
USAir	11,155,426
Western	10,380,774
Wein/Transtar	1,722,364
World	2,258,818

* Revenue Passenger-Miles (RPM) is one revenue passenger transported one mile in revenue service. This variable is equivalent to the revenue sales commonly used in manufacturing industries.
SOURCE: *Air Carrier Traffic Statistics*, 1986. Reprinted by permission.

over an 8-year period (from January 1979 to December 1986), served as the sample for the current research.

The primary data source for actions and responses was *Aviation Daily*, an industry journal with a 50-year history. A comprehensive investigation of *Aviation Daily* revealed that: (a) It had the most complete and detailed information for the purposes of this study; (b) it presented a very unbiased and representative reporting of competitive events; (c) it was not sensitive to the potential financial influences of airlines since it does not solicit their advertisements; and (d) it was not influenced by the need to create only newsworthy stories, for example, by only writing about the best known firms, as might be the case with a periodical marketed to the general public. The investigation of *Aviation Daily* included: extensive reviews of it relative to other publications, extending from general business publications, such as the *Wall Street Journal*, *Business Week*, and *Fortune*, to industry-specific publications, including *Aviation Week and Space Technology*, *Air Transport World*, and *Airline Executive*; interviews with its officials; and interviews with chief executive officers and members of the boards of directors of domestic airlines. In fact, *Aviation Daily* is an industry publication to which members of the industry (consultants, brokers, suppliers, and so on) subscribe on a yearly basis [2]. Other publications seem to merely duplicate the information found in *Aviation Daily*.

As noted, *competitive events* include both a market action and a response or responses to it. Competitive actions were considered significant and important only if they were mentioned in *Aviation Daily* and only if they were counteracted by at least one competitor. A response was identified by a key word search of each issue of *Aviation Daily*. Key words included "in responding to," "following," "under the pressure of," "reacting to," and the like. For example, *Aviation Daily* reported that "Under the pressure of American Airlines' planned hub creation, Piedmont revealed a statewide expansion program in Florida" (July 10, 1985). In this example Piedmont's Florida expansion was identified as responding to American Airlines' hub creation.

A rigorous procedure was followed to trace strings of actions and responses to identify the initial action. The procedure began by examining each daily issue of *Aviation Daily*, beginning with the last day of 1986. Employing the key word methodology, the researchers identified responses and traced back, day by day, over the 8 years, to find the reporting of the initial action. If, for example, on October 3, 1983, People's Express opened a new gate in response to Eastern's September 1 gate opening announcement, Eastern would be labeled the actor and People's Express would be identified as the responder. This combination would constitute a competitive event with one actor and one responder. However, if it was later reported that American reacted to Eastern's gate opening on November 25 by changing its route structure, then American would be the second responder behind People's Express. Thus, the methodology identifies first actors as well as all responders in their order of response to the initial action.

There were 191 competitive actions and 418 responses identified over the 8-year period. To confirm the validity of this procedure, a random sample of 20 events was constructed and verified by other major business publications. Of the 20 events, only 3 could not be completely confirmed, and this seemed to occur because the reporting of major airline events in other key press outlets was much less comprehensive than in *Aviation Daily*.

Study 4: Computer Retailing

The fourth study involved the fragmented computer retailing industry in the Washington Metropolitan area and was similar in design to Studies 1 and 2. The competitive responses of 25 computer retailers were examined to identify the factors that trigger some firms to respond. Mean sales volume for firms in the sample was $1.5 million, ranging from $80,000 to $80 million.

As in the earlier studies, the first step in the data-collection process was extensive interviewing of each firm's executive officers. Through the interviews the researchers were able to pinpoint meaningful ways of identifying actions and responses and the factors that explain why a firm responds to a rival's action. In addition, the interviews were helpful for gathering background data on each firm and for soliciting the support of each firm in the second phase of the study.

In the second phase a formal questionnaire was developed and administered to each CEO during the interview. CEOs were asked to identify an important *competitive action* in their industry to which their firm responded, as well as a *competitive action* to which their firm did not respond. Responses to a number of questions were then assessed to identify the factors that trigger a firm to respond.

Dynamic Measures of Competitive Actions and Responses

We will divide our discussion of dynamic measures into those focusing on either competitive responses or competitive actions. The bulk of the discussion is devoted to measures of response since these cut across each of the different chapters of the book. In terms of competitive response, we focused on issues of response imitation, response lag or time, response order, number of responders, and response likelihood.

Response imitation, or the degree to which a response imitated an action, was measured in terms of the concurrence of the action type and the response type. An imitation score was created to measure the degree of duplication involved in each response. This imitation score was calculated so that when the type of response was the same as the type of action (for example, a price cut in response to a price cut), the imitation score equaled 1; when the response type was not the same as the action type (for example, a price cut in response to a new product introduction), the imitation score equaled 0. The response imitation score was measured at the event unit of analysis, and it was also averaged across time for each competitor for each year. In the case of averaging, a high score for a firm would indicate a propensity to mimic or duplicate a competitor's action, whereas a low score would indicate the opposite.

Response lag was measured by the amount of time in days it took a firm to respond to a competitor's action. The amount of time was measured by the temporal difference between the dates of a specific competitive action and the response. Response lag was measured at the event unit of analysis and also averaged for each firm within a given year. Thus, if a firm responded four times in 1982 at response intervals of 10, 12, 14, and 16 days, each event could be used with scores of 10, 12, 14, and 16 days, or alternatively, its average response time for 1982, 13 days, could be employed in analyses.

Response order was measured by the rank position in time of the responding firm among all responders in an event. This was calculated by averaging a firm's actual rank position in the order of responders for each action for each year. For example, if a firm responded to three actions in 1985 and its order of response to these actions was 2nd, 4th, and 6th, its average response order for 1985 would be 4th.

Number of responders was defined as the total number of rivals who actually respond to an action. It was determined by counting the number of rivals; for example, a number 4 would indicate that four firms responded to a particular action.

Response likelihood was calculated by summing the number of times a firm responded to competitors' actions during a given year and dividing this figure by the number of times the firm had an opportunity to respond (this measure is unique to the airline study). For example, if a firm responded to 12 actions in 1983 and 2 actions in 1984, and it had opportunities to respond to 24 actions in 1983 and only 20 actions in 1984, its response likelihood would be .50 in 1983 and .10 in 1984. Consequently, firms that score high on this scale are more likely responders. Response opportunity was obtained by counting the number of actions that potentially affected each firm (there was no double counting). That is, if a price cut by a competitor was targeted at the markets of only 2 of its 10 rivals, only rivals operating in these markets would have an opportunity or sense a need to respond. Thus all of the competitors serving markets affected by an action would be counted since they would all have an opportunity to respond.[3]

In the area of competitive actions we studied the magnitude of the action, the scope of the action, the threat of the action, and the implementation requirements of the action. Measures of competitive actions are only briefly introduced here as these are discussed in more detail in Chapter 4. The *magnitude of an action* is defined as the extent of resources required to effectively implement an action. Some actions, such as a major new product introduction, require significantly more resources to implement than others, such as a new promotional campaign in a single market. The extent of resources required to implement an action was evaluated by a panel of experts.

The *scope of an action* is the number of competitors directly affected by the action. An action can have very wide scope, impacting all the competitors in an industry, or it can be of narrow scope, specifically targeting a single competitor. Scope of the action was measured in terms of the number of competitors potentially impacted by the action.

Threat of an action was defined and measured in terms of the number of customers an action could potentially steal from a rival. An action that has the potential to steal all of a competitor's customers would be considered very threatening. This variable was measured by counting the number of customers that could potentially be garnered by a rival's action.

The final action measure is *implementation requirement of an action*. It was measured by length of time between the announced date of an action and the precise date on which the action was implemented. Some actions are announced and implemented on the same day (e.g., a price cut), while other actions (e.g., the introduction of a new product) take considerably more time to implement.

Further, in addition to measures of actions and responses, the research also employs a number of macro organizational information measures, as well as macro performance measures. These include organizational variables such as external orientation, structure, slack, and decision making, and performance measures such as return on sales, return on assets, and sales growth. All of these will be defined and discussed as they are presented for analysis in the chapters which follow.

The use of macro measures, in conjunction with more micro dynamic measures, presents some interesting complications in the analysis. In particular, whereas actions and responses are at the event unit of analysis, macro measures of performance (e.g., return on equity) or information processing (e.g., slack resources) are often in aggregated macro form. Let us consider a firm that makes 15 responses during a given year. If the researcher wishes to explain the speed of these responses by organizational variables of the responding firm that are only measurable from year-end archival records (e.g. slack), or to see how these response times predict year-end performance (e.g., return on equity, again often only available from year-end financial statements), he or she must reconcile the differing unit of analysis. This reconciliation requires that the researcher aggregate response times into average composite scores (e.g., the average response lag for all 15 responses) or duplicate the macro organizational variable so that they match up with the event unit of analysis (e.g., duplicating the slack or performance measure times for the 15 events). This research will alternatively utilize both procedures, depending upon the research question and kinds of data under consideration. Each procedure has certain trade-offs, as our previous discussion suggests.

Summary

In this chapter we have considered the alternative methods for studying actions and responses. These range from primary methods, involving subjective inference, to more secondary methods often considered more objective. We have made clear the difficulties of studying actions and responses with any single method and have opted for a triangulation approach. Through triangulation, the researchers can establish that the results are not an artifact of any single method. Moreover, triangulation will provide a more complete, holistic, and contextual portrayal of the dynamics of competitive strategy.

In addition, this chapter has also highlighted the methodological procedures associated with each of the four studies. The methods range from case studies and panels of experts to archival sources, such as news media and corporate records. The dynamic action and response measures were next introduced and defined. Response measures include type of response, response lag, response imitation, response order, and number of responders. Action measures include magnitude of action, scope of action, threat of action, and implementation requirements of action. In Chapter 3 we will present the first segment of empirical results, focusing on the effects of characteristics of the acting firm on response.

Notes

1. For a discussion of the problems of retrospective reporting, the reader is referred to Huber and Power (1984).

2. *Aviation Daily*'s readership is composed of 36% air carriers; 32% air services and financial organizations; 21% air equipment manufacturers and distributors; and 11% government and airports.

3. Consider the methodological implications of market segmentation. The airline industry is segmented into a number of different geographic markets. With regard to the measurement of imitation, lag, and order, the segmentation of the industry poses no problem in that the methodology automatically selects segments where airlines are competing with one another. If a firm responds to another firm's actions, it is clear that they are competitors. For example, response lag for Northwest Airlines reflects the average speed of response to actions on segments where Northwest competes. Thus the methodology controls for the competition between certain market segments for these three measures.

However, it is important to account for the market segmentation in the response likelihood measure. That is, each airline competes in a selected set of geographic markets, with some airlines, such as United, present in most every market while others, such as America West, focus regionally. Thus, if United lowers prices only in its eastern routes, one would not expect America West to respond. Accordingly, the specific domestic airlines in the market affected by each competitive action were delineated. When measuring response likelihood for each airline, the methodology takes into consideration the number of times competitive actions occurred in that airline's markets. That is, the measure reflects the absolute number of actions to which a competitor would have a need or opportunity to respond.

3

Firm Reputation and Rivalry

FIRMS that undertake competitive actions possess different reputations and vary in terms of their credibility in the marketplace. Some firms may be viewed as "predators," frequently cutting prices to drive out rivals, while other firms may be regarded as "docile" for simply ignoring the actions of rivals. This chapter explores the critical role that a firm's reputation can exert in rivalry. The central argument is that a rival's reputation provides important information about its likely course of future competitive actions and reactions, and therefore this information can be very useful in competitor analysis. The chapter is unique in that it reports empirical research specifically designed to test relationships between firm reputation and the actions and responses of rivals to one another.

AUTHORS' NOTE: Leith Wain, a Ph.D. student at the University of Maryland, co-authored this chapter.

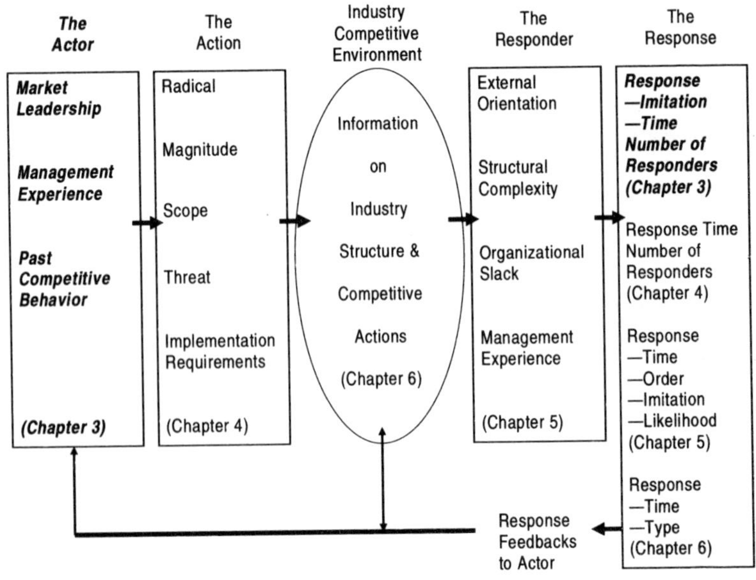

Figure 3.1. The Focus of Chapter 3

Figure 3.1 links the emphasis of this chapter on reputation of actors to the overall communication-information processing model presented in Chapter 1. In this chapter we first review the literature on firm reputation with the aim of identifying a set of firm-specific reputation indicators. Predictions of response characteristics based on firm-specific indicators of reputation are next offered, grounded in communication-information processing theory. Finally, the results are presented and discussed from the viewpoint of the manner in which reputation can be used to build competitive advantage.[1]

The Role of Firm Reputation in Rivalry

Reputation is defined as a positive or negative attribute ascribed to one rival by another based on past behavior (Wilson, 1985). Reputation can be both an asset and a liability: As an asset it can generate future economic profits (Shapiro, 1983); as a liability it can reveal information to competitors regarding future actions.

Firm reputation has been studied and modeled most extensively by economists who have long realized that multi-period models of rivalry would require the inclusion of reputations (Fellner, 1949; Scherer & Ross, 1990; Tirole, 1989). Moreover, the notion of using strategic actions to build a positive reputation has been explored in a variety of contexts, for example, reputation to deter future entry (Milgrom & Roberts, 1982; Yamey, 1972); reputation-generated price premiums (Shapiro, 1983); and reputation and information distribution (Kreps & Wilson, 1982a). Additionally, the role of reputation is recognized explicitly in contractual arrangements (Williamson, 1985) and organizational structure (Diamond, 1984).

More recently, reputation has been incorporated formally in game-theoretic models of rivalry (Tirole, 1989). Although early models focused on elimination of outcome uncertainty through the inclusion of information concerning bargainer attributes and the structure of the bargaining situation (Nash, 1950), recent extensions have included bargaining under incomplete information, thus allowing more realistic modeling of competitive interaction. For example, Kreps and Wilson (1982b) modeled sequential equilibria gaming under assumptions of incomplete information and proposed that each player's strategy is optimal, with respect to some rational assessment of probabilities of uncertain events, and dependent on beliefs concerning the other player's strategy. Wilson (1985) focused on the role of private information and players' expectations of each other in situations of repeated rivalry. In this regard, reputation emerged as the critical factor in the estimation of the likely course of action by different rivals.

Although an extensive theoretical literature on reputation has been developed, there has been little empirical work on the subject. One of the few papers is by Fombrun and Shanley (1990), who explore the link between a firm's reputation and such characteristics as performance, conformity to social norms, and strategy. This chapter builds on Fombrun and Shanley by investigating the impact of firm reputation on competitive interaction. More specifically, we use different indicators of the actor's reputation to predict a rival's response.

Recall from Chapter 1 that actors benefit from actions to which customers react favorably and where competitors cannot or do not respond. However, uncertainty about customer reactions and competitor responses often dominates this competitive setting. It is in this context that the reputations of firms can serve to lessen uncertainty for managers. For example, during the '50s and '60s Pepsi gained significant market share against Coca-Cola in the retail segment of the U.S. soft drink market. Customers responded favorably to Pepsi's actions, which included innovative TV advertising, investments in vertical integration, strengthening network distributors, and hiring TV personalities to represent Pepsi products. All during this time Coca-Cola ignored Pepsi, electing not to respond. Indeed, over the years, Coke had developed a reputation for never acknowledging its competition. Thus, it was relatively easy for the management of Pepsi to predict that Coke would not respond. Only when Pepsi became the market leader in the grocery segment of this industry did Coke respond.

The case of Kodak and Polaroid rivalry in instant photography provides another example of the important role that reputation can play in reducing uncertainty. It was certain to all industry observers in 1969 that Kodak was planning to enter the $600-million instant photography business, since Polaroid's patents had expired. In Polaroid's previous 18 years, its color film sales had grown to equal that of Kodak. However, Polaroid forced Kodak to introduce its EK 6 instant camera product too early by announcing its new product intentions (a threat). Kodak, in a race "to the market" with Polaroid, quickly entered but faced significant production problems, forcing its overall initial entry to be ineffective. Critically, Polaroid had a significant reputation for always rapidly and successfully expanding the quality and breadth of its product line after a new product was introduced. This reputation likely prompted Kodak, which had to be very fearful of being left behind again in the instant photography market, to move prematurely.

In the next section of this chapter we identify a number of information dimensions that capture different aspects of reputation. These include the reputation of the actor as a market leader, the reputation of the actor's top management team, and the actor's reputation as derived from its past competitive behavior. These reputation dimensions are used to predict characteristics of response, including the number of responders, response time, and degree of response imitation.

Informational Indicators of Reputation and Response

Reputation as a Market Share Leader

We hypothesize that the greater the reputation of the actor as a market share leader:

1. the greater the tendency for a rival to imitate the action;
2. the greater the number of rival responses to the action;
3. the faster the response times to the action.

The arguments for these relationships are as follows: High market share and high profitability are often viewed by managers as favorable outcomes of successfully conceived and well-executed organizational strategies. In fact, the explicit strategic implication of the growth share matrix is that high market share leads to profitability (Buzzell, Gale, & Sultan, 1975). Other studies have verified in general the correlation between market share and profitability (Prescott, Kohli, & Venkatramen, 1986; Zeithaml & Fry, 1984) and identified market share as a key organizational objective (Porter, 1979). Furthermore, Fombrun and Shanley (1990) noted that larger firms receive greater scrutiny than smaller firms, so managers tend to become disproportionately more familiar with the larger firms' activities. This enhanced familiarity tends to result in a market share leader being assigned a more favorable reputation than firms with smaller market shares.

Thus, firms that have achieved a high market share are watched closely and are considered leaders in that they have demonstrated successful expansionary capability as well as the ability to exploit market opportunities (Scherer & Ross, 1990). In this respect, high market share is associated with historical success within the industry, a demonstration of high growth, and an accumulation of significant organizational skills. Rival managers will attribute a competitor's high market share to skilled leadership. Additionally, they will devote increased attention to high market share firms, further enhancing the reputations of the market leaders.

Fellner (1949) noted that superiority of process, product, or sales techniques of the leading firm will confer increased relative strength to it by rivals because the superiority "testifies to fitness." In short, competing managers will tend to attribute a high probability of success to the actions of a market leader and will respond accordingly. Fellner also notes that manifestations of market superiority may be "interpreted as a sign of ruthlessness" by rival firms. The achievement of a high market share by one firm is often accomplished at direct cost to other firms competing for the same resources (Scherer & Ross, 1990). The zero sum nature of such interaction conveys an aggressive reputation to those firms that actively compete for market share; the winner is ruthless by default, having cannibalized market share from its rivals and in the process demonstrated market leadership. Thus, the actions of a market leader will be interpreted by rivals as "ideal" and consistent with an aggressive market leadership role.

These arguments about the market share leader parallel those on opinion leadership in the communication literature (e.g., Rogers, 1983). Opinion leadership concerns the degree to which an actor informally influences the opinion of potential followers/responders through its position as industry leader. In short, opinion leaders serve as a paragon to which followers will aspire, exemplifying the norms of correct industry behavior. For example, IBM might be considered an opinion leader among computer companies, and American Airlines among airlines.

In summary, high market share leaders will be more visible in the marketplace, and thus competitors will have more information and be more knowledgeable about their activities, in contrast to those of small firms that are less visible. Opinion leaders will probably have more experience in knowing when and how to act and therefore will be given greater credibility. Accordingly, actions by market share leaders will prompt an increase in the tendency for a response to imitate the action, an increased number of competitive responses, and faster response times.

Reputation Based on Management Team Characteristics

Just as high market share may connote a leadership effect for a firm, so too can the experience and composition of the top management team. We predict that the greater the top management team's reputation for predictability:

1. the lower the number of rival responses;
2. the less the rival imitation of a rival's actions;
3. the slower the response times.

Lubatkin, Chung, Rogers, and Owers (1989) found that stockholders react positively or negatively to CEO successions based on the reputational attributes of the incoming individual. Rival managers, in a similar manner, can observe reputation information on the composition and experience of the top management teams of firms and gain insight into their expected strategic behavior. Porter (1980) argues that the educational institutions and work organizations in which a rival's managers have been trained and socialized are predictive of future moves, as are managers' previous track records and personal successes and failures.

Future competitive behavior can become very predictable for top management teams with significant within-industry experience. More experienced teams will tend to follow the status quo, earning a less aggressive reputation, than will those with little industry experience (Hambrick & Mason, 1984). For example, Porter observes that managers with long tenure will often reuse ideas that have worked well in the past, and in the process will become quite predictable. On the other hand, teams that lack experience will be more unpredictable; they will not have a track record through which rivals can reduce uncertainty by inferring competitive intentions (Oster, 1990; Porter, 1980). Some organizations even incorporate such unpredictable behavior in their strategic thrusts; Bic Pen followed an explicit human resources policy of hiring from outside the industry because it wanted its competitive strategy to be unpredictable (Porter, 1980).

Reputation Based on Previous Competitive Behavior

Observation of past actions can provide insight into future behavior (Oster, 1990; Weigelt and Camerer, 1988). A firm must act consistently to achieve long-term goals (Andrews, 1980). To the extent that firm actions are consistent, or "reliable," managers of rivals will award the firm a reputation for consistency or predictability. For example, a large firm may be described as a "sleeping giant" if it has been predominantly inactive in rivalry, or it may be awarded a reputation as "aggressive" if it has demonstrated a predilection for aggressive price-cutting (Oster, 1990). As we have noted, the reputation developed from past competitive actions can be extremely useful in predicting future actions.

We predict that the greater the reputation of the actor as an aggressive price predator:

1. the greater the number of rival responses to its actions;
2. the greater the rival imitation of its actions;
3. the faster the response times.

Firms that have a history of taking aggressive actions will be viewed by rivals as aggressive predators (Oster, 1990). The goals of such actions will be clear: aggressively gain share or aggressively defend share. With such unambiguous information on intentions, rivals must be prepared to react just as aggressively. Thus actors with predatory pricing reputations will be more likely to evoke rival reactions that will be similarly aggressive: fast, numerous, and imitative. Responses will tend to be imitative to avoid escalating the competitive battle.

In contrast to the predatory aggressive reputation, rivals can develop a reputation for taking actions of greater magnitude, often referred to as strategic actions. These firms can easily develop reputations as strategic players. A history of actions of major magnitude implies a certain complexity in strategic behavior. Firms must make some assessment of their rival's future competitive behavior; this is a far more difficult task when studying a firm that has taken frequent complex actions, as opposed to a firm that has mainly taken price actions. Frequent pricing actions generally represent the competitive actualization of an underlying "incremental change" strategy, whereas actions of major magnitude imply fundamental changes in firm strategy (Lindblom, 1959). Therefore, firms that alter prices frequently, but do not engage in strategic actions, can be viewed as having demonstrated greater strategic consistency (Miller & Friesen, 1984). In contrast, it will be more difficult to predict the behavior of firms that are continuously altering their strategies in a fundamental way. Therefore, we predict that the greater the reputation of the actor as a strategic player:

1. the fewer the number of rival responses to its actions;
2. the less the rival imitation of its actions;
3. the slower the response times to its actions.

Table 3.1 summarizes the hypotheses to be tested: the relationship between the reputation indicators, the information these indicators are theorized to represent, and the predictions regarding response.

Table 3.1 Hypotheses: Summary of Reputation Indicators, the Information These Indicators Are Theorized to Represent, and the Predictions Regarding Response

Reputation Indicator	*Information Content*	*Competitive Response Prediction*
High Market Share of Actor	leadership, opinion leader, aggressive	more imitation, faster response time, higher number of responders
Long Tenure and High Management Experience of Actor's Management Team	follower of status quo; more predictable	fewer number of responders, slower response times, less imitation
History as a Price-Cutter	predator, aggressive, and threatening	higher imitation, faster response time, higher number of responders
History as a Strategic Player	complex actions, risky, and unpredictable	fewer number of responders, slower response times, less imitation

Measures

Market leader reputation was inferred from the actor's market share in a given year. High market share would suggest a market leader. The market share of each acting firm was determined by the proportion of total industry operating revenues generated by the specific firm. Revenue data were gathered on an annualized basis for each airline, for each year, from the *Air Carrier Financial Statistics.*

Management reputation of the actor was measured in terms of the top management team's demographic data. The average number of years of within-industry experience of the top management team for each airline was calculated from corporate executive listings in the *Dun and Bradstreet Corporate Directory* and used in this research. Note that this measure is highly correlated with age and inversely correlated with level of education. The top management team was defined as all executives listed in the directory. The chief executive officer was selected, and seven other corporate executives listed in the directory were randomly chosen for each airline (there were on average 22 corporate airline executives listed in Dun and Bradstreet for each airline), for each year, and data were gathered on the industry experience of each.

The actor's reputation as a strategic player and/or predatory price-cutter was assessed in terms of its action history during the preceding year. Lagging the action history data by one year captured the historical nature of firm reputation and its subsequent impact on competitive responses. Strategic actions were defined as significant commitments of unique resources that are difficult to implement and reverse (Chen, 1988), and include actions such as mergers, new product introductions, and new hub openings. All of the strategic actions during each preceding year were summed for each actor, to proxy each actor's reputation as a strategic player. The number of pricing actions in the preceding year were also summed for each actor to reflect the actor's total predilection to act as a pricing predator.

The three response measures were consistent with the definitions provided in Chapter 2. Briefly, *response likelihood* is the expectation of a competitive response to each identified competitive action where the probability of a response is divided by the probability of no response. *Response imitation* is the degree of concurrence of the action type and the response type. For example, when a price cut is made in response to a price cut, the imitation score equaled 1; when the response type was not the same as the action type, the imitation score equaled 0. *Response lag* is the temporal difference between the date of a specific competitive action and when the response occurred. *Number of responders* was measured as the aggregate number of responders by all rivals to a given competitive action. The *n* for imitation and response times is based on the number of responses in the sample ($N = 378$; note some actions had multiple

Table 3.2 Correlations Among Major Variables[a]

Variables	*1*	*2*	*3*	*4*	*5*	*6*
1. Imitation						
2. Number of Responders	.09					
3. Speed of Response	−.03	.14*				
4. Team Experience	.10*	−.11	.15***			
5. Strategic Actions	−.11*	−.07	.27***	.05		
6. Pricing Actions	.20***	.11	−.17***	−.16***	−.10*	
7. Market Share	.33***	.22***	.05	.11*	.14**	.10*

[a] for variable (2) $N = 119$; for all other variables, $N = 378$.
*$p<.05$
**$p<.01$
***$p<.001$

responses); the n for number of responders is based on the number of actions in the sample that elicited at least one response (n = 119).

Data Analysis and Findings

Table 3.2 reports the correlations, and Table 3.3 reports the regression results. Separate regression models were run with imitation, number of responders, and response time as dependent variables. Overall examination of the results yielded general support that competitive response can, at least partly, be predicted by the actor's reputation.

Model (1) regressed response time against the reputation variables. The results suggest that a rival firm's speed of response is at least partially a function of the reputation of the acting firm's top management team and its past history as a strategic player and price predator. In particular, a reputation of the acting firm's top management team for predictability or a lack of aggressiveness (more tenure) is associated with a slower response by rival firms. Additionally, the greater the reputation of the acting firm as a strategic player, the slower the responses of rivals. Furthermore, actors with reputations as

Table 3.3 Results of Regression Analysis[a]

Variables	*Imitation*[b]	*Speed of Response*[b]	*Number of Responders*[c]
Intercept	0.734***	–2.540	3.136***
	(0.089)	(4.000)	(0.693)
Market Share	1.974***	7.397	8.592***
	(0.310)	(17.394)	(2.527)
Average Industry Experience	0.003	0.611**	–0.071**
	(0.004)	(0.215)	(0.029)
Strategic Player	–0.062**	4.499***	–0.063
	(0.025)	(1.402)	(0.194)
Price Predator	–0.034***	–0.954*	0.024
	(0.009)	(0.518)	(0.075)
R^2	0.123	0.063	0.086
F-test	12.993***	6.316***	4.017**

[a] Standard errors appear in parentheses.
[b] $N = 378$
[c] $n = 119$
*$p<.05$
**$p<.01$
***$p<.001$

aggressive price predators elicited responses from rivals more rapidly than did actors without this reputation. The market leader reputation of the actor was unrelated to response time.

Model (2) regressed the average number of responders to a competitive action against firm reputation. The number of responders to competitive actions was partially predicted by the market leader reputation of the acting firm and the reputation of the top management team. Specifically, and as predicted, the greater the leadership reputation of the acting firm, the greater the number of rival responses to its actions. Also, fewer firms responded to actors possessing top management teams with a reputation for predictability and a lack of aggressiveness. A firm's history of past action was unrelated to the number of responses to its actions.

Model (3) regressed the imitation variable against firm reputation. The results suggest that the greater the market leader reputation of the acting firm, the more likely the responding firms will imitate. Additionally, the greater the reputation of the acting firm as a strategic player, the less likely it was for responders to imitate its actions. However, and contrary to expectations, the greater the reputation of an actor as an aggressive price predator, the less the imitation of the action. This result was opposite the direction expected. Imitation was unrelated to the reputation of the top management team.

Overall, the four independent reputation variables account for 12% of the variation in response imitation ($F = 12.99$; $p<.000$), 6% of the variation in response time ($F = 6.32$; $p<.000$), and 9% of the variation in number of responders ($F = 4.02$; $p<.003$).

Discussion

The purpose of this chapter was to test relationships between reputation and response. The results suggest that firm reputation plays an important role in determining the way a rival will respond.

Past game-theoretic models and strategic management research have identified the role of reputation in competitive interaction and have pointed to its importance in determining the probability and nature of rival responses to competitive actions. This chapter emphasized direct observation of the competitive actors and the associated effect of firm reputation on the responses of rivals.

Although preliminary, the research begins to contribute to a theory of reputation. Indeed, the results are path-breaking in highlighting the important role of firm reputation in rivalry. From a theoretical perspective, the linkage of past action history, firm attributes, and management reputation to response characteristics offers important support for the conceptual correlation between firm reputation and future market opportunities, and directly contributes to a theory of competitor analysis.

Consistent with the notion that market achievement connotes a favorable reputation, market share leadership was associated with imitative response behavior by rival firms. Additionally, market leaders can expect responses from more than one rival.

Top management team reputation of the acting firm was also an important predictor. Indeed, top management teams with an unpredictable reputation (teams with less industry experience) were more likely to evoke fast responses than more predictable teams. Furthermore, and as expected, predictable top management teams (teams with lengthy industry experience) generated fewer rival responses to their competitive actions than teams with less established reputations. It should be noted that experience level was highly correlated with age and educational level. In this regard the research suggests that rivals will aggressively respond to the actions of firms with younger and more educated management teams.

Consistent with the notion that reputation is based on observed data and has utility as a predictor of future actions, the reputation of a firm as a strategic player and/or price actor was an important determinant of how quickly rivals responded to competitive actions, and whether their responses were imitative. As a firm's reputation as a strategic player increased, rivals took more time to respond. The timing results are generally consistent with the notion that strategic players design actions that are complex and difficult to duplicate. Furthermore, the imitation of actions by players with strategic reputations is less than that for firms without such a reputation. This result was expected since strategic players often undertake complex actions that are more difficult to duplicate.

A reputation as an aggressive price predator generated the expected rapid responses by rivals. However, contrary to expectations, the responses were less likely to be imitative. One possible explanation for this result may rest with management's reluctance to compete directly with a firm holding a price predator reputation. Managers of rival firms, noting the actor's reputation for taking frequent aggressive pricing actions, may recognize the need for quick responses, but fear the consequences of matching the action with an identical response. An initial price cut taken by a firm with a recognized predilection for such action, if countered with a similar price cut, may quickly escalate into an extended price war, with associated loss of profits for all affected firms (Oster, 1990). By responding quickly, the responding firm demonstrates its willingness and capability to engage in competitive warfare. However, by not imitating the action, the responder potentially avoids the prospect of sequential price-cutting.

Future Research Questions

This study examined several measures of reputation and demonstrated that they influence competitive interaction and rival responses. Although it seems intuitive that rival firms assess each other's reputations, and theory suggests that rivals make decisions based in part on this assessment, many issues surround the identification and measurement of reputation. Future research possibilities revolve around the conditions that make reputation an asset or liability, the identification and measurement of additional reputational indicators, replication of findings in other industries, and additional fieldwork to determine what variables managers actually use in assessing the reputations of rivals. Table 3.4 presents a lists of research questions for future study. We now discuss each of these questions.

As noted previously, reputation can be both an asset and a liability to a firm. As an asset it may act to impede a rival's reaction; as a liability it may reveal private information, thus enhancing a rival's position. The present research suggests that a firm's competitive position is enhanced by having a management team with many years of experience (a management team reputation for predictability) and by having a reputation as a strategic player. Competitive responses in general appear to be less intense when such reputational characteristics are operative; thus, investments in these characteristics of reputation could be considered a worthwhile asset or goal. Interestingly, having a reputation as a market share leader and price predator

Table 3.4 Future Reputation/Rivalry Research Questions

1. What features of reputation serve as an asset and a liability for firms?
2. What are the trade-offs that firms must make in taking actions that lead to short-term positive performance outcomes but negative reputational outcomes?
3. Should managers actively invest in reputation?
4. What is the influence of other reputation indicators, such as slack resources, social consciousness, and history of competitive retribution, on the characteristics of response?
5. To what extent are reputation effects industry-specific?
6. To what extent can the reputation developed in one industry be used in another?
7. To what extent do/should managers actually assess the reputation of rivals?
8. What variables do managers utilize to make their assessments of a rival's reputation?

appears to intensify rivalry, thus potentially serving as a liability for actors. Researchers need to better understand the conditions under which some aspects of reputation constitute an asset or liability. Consider the case of the firm attempting to develop an aggressive price-cutting reputation to deter a rival's move. Oster (1990) argues that cutting prices to develop a reputation can be expensive since it may entail significant short-term losses. A less expensive scheme would be to keep prices high but threaten to cut prices if a rival's move were to occur. However, a threat must be credible to be effective. Oster notes that: "If you threaten an action which will not be profitable, for that threat to be credible you must somehow 'guarantee' that you will follow through" (p. 265). This can be achieved by *investments* that enhance credibility or reputation. For example, a firm that has cut prices significantly after competitors imitated its move would develop a reputation over time as an aggressive price-cutter (Milgrom & Roberts, 1982). This reputation could be used in the future by the acting firm to influence potential responders in their decision to respond or not. That is, a future threat would now be credible because of the reputation developed from past price-cutting actions. From the actor's perspective, the past price-cutting could be seen as an investment that would have short-term negative consequences (lower profits) but long-term positive consequences (less rivalry and higher profits). Rivals interested in maximizing their profits could be deterred from acting because to do so would lead to a price war and lower profits.

Moreover, a firm that had made significant investments in plant capacity, or had invested in keeping a significant cash reserve on hand, might present a credible threat to cut prices. Excess plant capacity would provide an incentive to more fully utilize capacity, and idle cash resources might mean that a firm was prepared to sustain a price war. The price-cut threat would be credible under these conditions because of past investments in either plant capacity or slack resources.

In the above example, we see how a firm can use investments in reputation as an asset to provide a credible threat to rivals; however, reputation can also be a liability by revealing private information. Take the case of the actor who is introducing a new product to the market for the first time. Since this actor has no experience in the introduction of new products, and thus no reputation, it may pay for rivals to take a wait-and-see attitude, delaying response until the overall market reaction can be assessed. If the new product failed to generate demand, no response would be necessary. If, on the other hand, this firm has a significant history of successful new product introductions, it might be reasonable to conclude that there will be a continued positive market reaction to its actions and that an immediate response is in order. Here the reputation of firms is used to reduce the market uncertainty for rival firms and can be considered a liability.

Similarly, rivals who have a reputation of always imitating the action of firms may prompt the acting firm to build barriers to imitation or to undertake actions secretly. Again, firm reputation in this case serves as a liability.

Thus, reputations, which are developed over time from past actions and behaviors, can be usefully thought of as investments. As such, they act as both an asset and a liability in the way they reduce uncertainty for firms.

This chapter utilized four informational indicators of reputation that were deemed observable by rival managers and likely to contribute to a theory of reputation; however, more theoretical work is needed to identify other informational variables that are likely to reflect firm reputation. Other indicators include organizational slack, social consciousness, and history of competitive retribution. As more variables are identified, a comprehensive model of reputation can be constructed, thus aiding more exhaustive and refined empirical studies.

Further, the domestic airline industry offered the opportunity to study reputation in an environment dominated by single-business firms. However, as an extension to this research, replication of findings among multibusiness and multinational firms is necessary before generalizing these results. A key question is whether reputation is industry-specific or, alternatively, whether a reputation made in one industry can be used successfully in another. The identification of a set of generic reputational variables would enhance the normative value of such research as well.

Finally, the question still exists as to the degree to which managers actually assess reputations, and if they do, what variables they actually utilize to make their assessments. Future research to determine the relationship between direct managerial assessment of reputation and its impact on decision making is needed to more accurately model the effect of reputation on competitive interaction.

Note

1. All relationships are tested in this chapter with longitudinal airline data on actions and response. See Chapter 2 for the description of the research method.

4

Competitive Actions and Rivalry

FIRMS build and defend their competitive advantage by undertaking various actions. For example, a firm can seek to improve its competitive position by the *act* of introducing a revolutionary new patent-protected product. The patent may be effective in blocking rivals' responses, as in the case of the

AUTHORS' NOTE: Portions of this chapter were adapted from: (a) "Action Characteristics as Predictors of Competitive Responses" by M. J. Chen, K. G. Smith, and C. Grimm, in press, *Management Science, 38*(3), pp. 439-455. Copyright 1992 by Institute of Management Sciences. Adapted by permission. (b) "Competitive Moves and Responses Among High-Technology Firms" by K. G. Smith, M. Gannon, and C. Grimm, in *The Handbook of Strategy* (ch. 31, p. 1) by Harold Glass (Ed.), 1990, New York: Warren, Gorham & Lamont. Copyright 1989 by Warren, Gorham & Lamont, Inc. Adapted by permission. (c) "Predictors of Response Time to Competitive Strategic Actions: Preliminary Theory and Evidence" by K. G. Smith, C. Grimm, M. J. Chen, and M. Gannon, 1989, *Journal of Business Research, 18*, p. 245-258. Copyright 1989 by Elsevier Science Publishing Company, Inc. Adapted by permission.

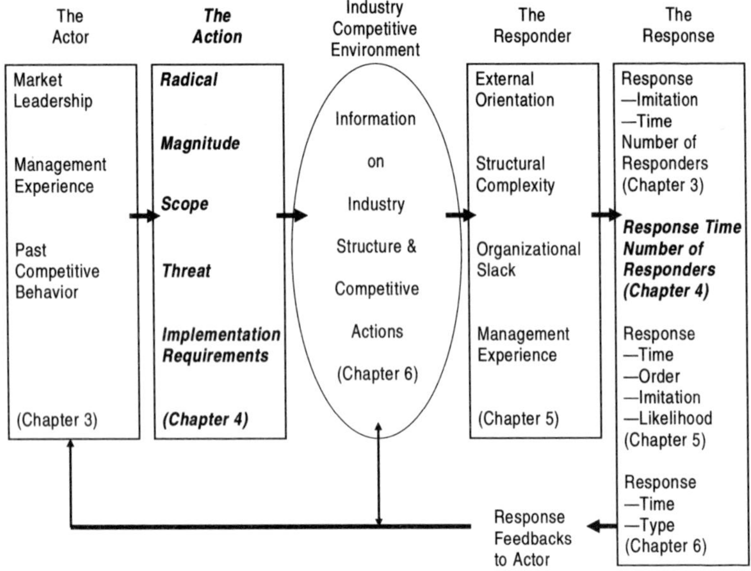

Figure 4.1. The Focus of Chapter 4

first instant photography camera created by Polaroid. Still another firm may successfully defend its advantage by *acting* to cut prices. In the early 1900s, Standard Oil weakened its rivals by drastically cutting prices in markets in which its competitors operated. Once competitors were weakened by this price-cutting, Standard Oil increased market share by acquiring these rivals. As these examples suggest, a firm's actions can be the building blocks of competitive advantage and, accordingly, can provide a powerful stimulus to competition.

This chapter examines the critical role of competitive actions in rivalry. A competitive action is defined as a specific and observable competitive move, such as a price cut or a new product introduction, initiated by a firm to defend or improve its relative competitive position (Chen, 1988). Figure 4.1 links the emphasis of this chapter on competitive actions to the overall organizational information model outlined in Chapter 1. The central argument of the chapter is that a firm's actions serve as a message to rival firms, providing important information that helps to determine the nature of response.

In the first section of this chapter we review the literature and research on competitive actions. Then we identify specific action characteristics and use these characteristics to predict the level of competitive rivalry. Finally, we test the predictions with data from all four of the major studies.

Competitive Actions

As noted in Chapter 1, the emphasis on competitive actions and responses is rooted in the writings of Schumpeter (1934, 1950), who viewed the market as a mechanism whereby firms experiment in taking specific actions; some firms undertake actions in a clear and explicit attempt to lead, while others simply follow and imitate. Firms successful in carrying out these actions (seizing opportunities) reap significant economic profits because of the monopolistic position awarded to them by the imitator's lag (Nelson & Winter, 1982). However, a long-term equilibrium is never reached. The excess profits of the acting firm and the losses or lost opportunities experienced by the non-responder motivate the latter to respond, perhaps imitating the action.

Schumpeter also emphasized the importance of economic profits in motivating a firm to act or respond. In theory, the acting firm can earn abnormal profits due to its monopolistic position prior to a response (the first mover advantage). This is not to imply, however, that all actions will lead to successful outcomes or that all actions will prompt a response. Rather, the argument is that when a firm's action generates above-normal economic profits, the responses of rivals can be anticipated because they will wish to share in the profits. Moreover, it is expected that as the profits derived from an action increase, so too will the speed and number of responders who will attempt to mimic or duplicate the action.

There has been a significant amount of research on competitive actions and rivalry, which can be classified into three general areas. Two areas of research have emphasized two very different types of competitive moves: pricing and product actions. The third area of research has focused on a firm's advertising actions designed to differentiate the product or service from the products or services of rivals. We will discuss each of these three areas sequentially.

Research on pricing actions has been dominated by industrial organization and game theory economists. Key issues on pricing and rivalry have included the effects of cutthroat pricing (Porter, 1985; Reynolds, 1940; Zucker, 1965), price collusion (Bishop, 1960; Fellner, 1949; Osborne & Pitchik, 1983; R. Porter, 1983), predatory pricing (Kreps & Wilson, 1982b; Milgrom & Roberts, 1982), and price leadership (Bain, 1960; Markham, 1951; Rotemberg & Saloner, 1985; Stigler, 1947). Some of the major findings of this research are: Firms are generally worse off financially after engaging in full-blown price competition (Porter, 1980); factors, such as few competitors, homogeneous cost structures, healthy industries, and good public information on firms, facilitate price collusion (Scherer & Ross, 1990); firms can use the threat of cutting prices to deter entry by rivals (Oster, 1990); and industry leaders often effectively limit price warfare by enacting pricing standards (Scherer & Ross, 1990).

The research on product actions and rivalry has generally emphasized two key topics: patents to prevent duplication (Levin, Klevorick, Nelson, & Winter, 1987; Mansfield, 1985; Mansfield, Schwartz, & Wagner, 1981) and being first with a product or service innovation (Baldwin & Childs, 1969; Eaton & Lipsey, 1981; Schnaars, 1986; Shaw & Shaw, 1984). The major conclusion of much of this research is that the effect of product/service actions on rivalry is contingent on firm and industry characteristics. For example, Levin et al. (1987) found that patents increased a rival's imitation costs by 40% for pharmaceuticals, by 25% for chemical products, and by 7% to 15% for semiconductors. In fact, timely duplication of major patented new products was reported in all but 12 of 127 industries. In addition, Mansfield (1985) found that large firms tend to imitate better than small firms. Moreover, Lieberman and Montgomery (1988), although noting that first mover advantages often do exist, highlight a set of conditions under which they do not.

There has also been a significant amount of research on the effectiveness of advertising actions designed to differentiate the product or service from those of rivals (Bond & Lean, 1979; Buzzell & Ferris, 1977; Robinson & Fornell, 1985; Schmalensee, 1972; Taylor & Weiserbs, 1972). The basic conclusion of this research is that it is not enough to simply advertise vigorously. Rather, some *act of innovation* in the product advertised and/or in the advertising itself is needed to create an advantage over rivals (Scherer & Ross, 1990).

While this research has provided significant insight into the relationship between competitive actions and rivalry, a relatively new and different perspective on competitive actions is evolving in strategic management. The underlying assumption behind this new stream of research is that competitive actions can best be understood by examining their underlying characteristics (MacMillan, 1983; MacMillan, McCaffrey, & Van Wijk, 1985). That is, not all competitive actions are alike, and characteristics of actions can themselves be important predictors of responses. Prominent action characteristics that have been found to influence rivalry include the visibility of an action and its competitive impact and radicality (MacMillan et al., 1985). These characteristics will be discussed below.

This new stream of research focusing on action characteristics offers a number of advantages. Most important, the study of action characteristics can directly contribute to a generalizable theory of competitive advantage. For example, characteristics of action that predict the speed of response and the number of responders can provide direct insight to managers attempting to design actions that will impede response. Moreover, because this action characteristic perspective is broader and more integrative than the stream of research in industrial organization economics or marketing, it allows researchers to draw on a variety of different theoretical perspectives. Furthermore, previous approaches to the study of competitive action and rivalry (e.g., type of action) can be readily subsumed under this emphasis on action characteristics. Finally, an action characteristic perspective allows for more meaningful cross-industry comparisons, as discussed more fully in Chapter 6.

Action Characteristics, Information, and Rivalry

From an information-processing point of view, a competitor's action carries a message, expressed or implied, that firms must process in order to compete successfully. For example, a significant across-the-board price cut by a major airline could be considered a broad action impacting many rivals. Rivals can easily categorize the intentions of such an action as aggressive, and its consequences are fairly easy to predict. In contrast, an airline could merge with a small commuter airline. The purpose for such an action will be more difficult for rivals to determine, and the market consequences would be more uncertain.

From a strategic management perspective, information carried in a competitor's action can act as a stimulus to rivals, leading to either an opportunity or a threat (Huber, 1982; Huber & Daft, 1987). Porter (1980) describes this form of communication as follows:

> The behavior of competitors provides signals in a myriad of ways. Some signals are bluffs, some are warnings, and some are earnest commitments to a course of action. Market signals are indirect means of communicating in the market place, and most if not all of a competitor's behavior can carry information that can aid in competitor analysis and strategy formulation. (p. 75)

Thus, just as individual communicators must try to understand both the implicit and the explicit meaning of the messages they send to one another, firms must attempt to understand the meaning and intent of rivals' actions. One way to derive meaning from a rival's move is to break down the action into its basic characteristics and then evaluate the information content of each characteristic. In this chapter we consider five action characteristics: the magnitude of the action, its scope, the degree of threat in the action, the extent to which the action is perceived by rivals as radical, and its implementation requirements. We discuss each of these in turn.

Action Magnitude

Some actions involve major commitments of resources for a firm, while others involve relatively few resources. The magnitude of an action refers to the extent to which resources are required to carry out and implement the action. As these resources increase, so too will the difficulty in reversing the action once its implementation has begun. This outcome will have the effect of increasing the total amount of risk for the acting firm. Therefore, actions of grand magnitude will be considered risky since they involve significant commitments of resources and are difficult to reverse. Because such actions often have important consequences for the firm, they can be considered strategic (Egelhoff, 1982; Porter, 1980, 1985; Smith & Grimm, 1987). Examples of strategic actions include the introduction of a new product or a major change in the definition of the business. In contrast, actions of lower magnitude are less risky because they involve fewer resources and are easier to reverse. Since these actions are often designed to fine-tune strategy, they can be considered tactical. Examples of tactical actions include price cuts and new advertising promotions.

In general, we hypothesize that the degree to which a firm pursues strategic actions will be negatively related to the number of responders and positively related to response lag. That is, major actions will provoke fewer and slower responses than minor actions. The logic for this prediction is that strategic actions, which involve significant commitments of resources, will be difficult for rivals to match. In particular, firms will be less likely to respond to strategic actions because the information contained in them may, at least initially, be unfamiliar and uncertain. For example, when a competitor introduces a new product, it is often unclear how successful such a product will be. Thus firms may prefer to take a "wait and see" attitude until information becomes more certain, so that responses to major actions will be relatively few and slow.

In contrast, firms will be more familiar with the information contained in tactical actions because they will likely have information from past experiences on which to base response decisions. For example, minor pricing actions are a common occurrence in most industries, and managers generally develop experience in responding to them. Accordingly, rivals will be more likely to respond and, on average, they will be more capable of responding quickly to low-magnitude actions than to high-magnitude actions.

Action Scope

The scope of the action refers to the number of targeted competitors that can be potentially affected. Some moves affect only one competitor, while others have greater scope, impacting many competitors. In general, we hypothesize that the scope of a firm's actions will be positively related to the number of responders and negatively related to response lag. That is, as the scope of an action increases, the number of responders and the speed of their responses will increase. Competitors affected directly by an action are most likely to be potential responders. From an information-processing point of view, as the number of competitors impacted by an action increases, so will the information about the action. The greater the information availability, the more likely it is that at least one rival will process this information and respond. Therefore, as the number of competitors impacted by an action increases, so does the likelihood of a response.

This will be true even in cases involving actions that are undertaken secretly. An action with a wide scope will require greater human resources to carry out and thus, as the scope of the action increases, will increase the potential for information leakage surrounding the implementation of a secret action. The greater the information leakage, the more likely competitors will learn of and respond to the action.

Consequently, competitors are more likely to become aware of and motivated to respond to an action of broad scope. Indeed, the very scale of the action may impel them to react. Moreover, once a few competitors have responded, others will tend to follow suit, creating a snowball effect (Porter, 1984). By the same token an action of wide scope that impacts many competitors will tend to provoke a relatively speedy response. Just as more competitors are likely to respond, so too is it likely that their responses will be faster. MacMillan et al. (1985) found that the broader the impact of a new product in the commercial banking industry, the shorter the competitors' response times.

Competitive Threat

Another characteristic of an action is the extent to which the action directly threatens a competitor's markets. That is, it is important not only to gauge the magnitude and scope of an action but also to assess the degree to which the action is designed to directly threaten a rival's customers. For example, a price cut would be perceived as quite threatening if it were large and/or targeted at a high percentage of a firm's customers.

Broadly speaking, the competitive threat of an action will be positively related to the number of responders and negatively related to response lag. More specifically, as the threat of an action increases, so will the number of responders and the speed of their responses. Firms will be less perceptive about information on actions that do not specifically affect them. However, when a rival directly targets the customers of a firm, that firm will become much more sensitized to the action. As a result, the firm will diligently analyze the available information on the action. Moreover, when many of a firm's customers are targeted by a rival's action, the firm is likely to receive a good amount of information about the move. For example, rather than directly switching suppliers following a price cut, customers may inquire to see if the current supplier will match the reduced price. From an information-processing point of view, then, as the threat of an action increases, so will the available information to and information-processing activities of the affected firm. Assuming the information is reliable (the threat is real), as the information about an action increases, so does the probability of a response.

Dutton and Jackson (1987) argued that managers are more likely to respond aggressively to actions perceived as threats than as opportunities. Thus, if an action simultaneously attempts to steal the customers of many competitors, these competitors would be forced to analyze the action and react. Porter (1980) contends that competitors will react quickly to threatening actions out of fear. In this regard, MacMillan et al. (1985) found that the greater the threat of an action to a firm, the faster its response time.

Radicality

An action that is new and entirely different from previous competitive moves in an industry can be considered radical (MacMillan et al.). We predict that the radicality of an action will be negatively related to the number of responders and positively related to response lag. That is, as the radicality of an action increases, responses will be fewer and slower.

Information surrounding actions that are radically different from past norms and operating assumptions in an industry will be more uncertain (MacMillan et al., 1985). Managers will not be able to use the information derived from past experiences to evaluate the action. Porter (1980) argued that actions defying the goals and assumptions of the industry will carry lengthy response times because competitors will not perceive the need for a response. Therefore, he argued that the best kinds of actions for a firm to take are those that defy the industry norms. MacMillan et al. found that the more an action was perceived as departing from industry norms, the longer the response times. Thus, in an information-processing sense, competitors will not have the information to properly evaluate a radical action. With less information we can expect fewer and slower responders.

Action Implementation Requirements

Finally, the action's implementation requirements or the extent of organizational effort required to implement an action may also be crucial to predicting response. In general, some level of commitment is necessary to facilitate interdepartmental coordination, reorganize existing procedures and policies, and train personnel in order to successfully implement an action (Galbraith, 1977). The action's implementation requirement can be measured by the time between the decision to act and the implementation of the action.

Generally speaking, we expect that an action's implementation requirement will be negatively related to the number of responders and positively related to response lag. That is, as the implementation requirement of an action increases, responses will be fewer and slower. If one assumes that competitors are similar in terms of organizational capabilities, then a rival's difficulty in implementing a response should at least be equal to that of the actors in implementing the initial move. Indeed, the responders may be at a disadvantage when reacting to a move. They would need time to understand the action and then properly design a response. Some rivals may lack the organizational capability to implement the necessary response, even if they have decided to do so. This may be especially true for actions characterized by very high implementation requirements. Thus, designing actions so that they are difficult to implement can work as an important barrier to response. In an information-processing sense, the likelihood of communication breakdowns and overload increases as firms attempt to carry out more difficult actions. This would have the effect of lessening the number of responders and the speed of response.

Table 4.1 summarizes the hypotheses to be tested: the relationships between the action characteristics, the information

Table 4.1 Hypotheses: Summary of Action Characteristics, the Information They Reflect and the Predicted Influence on Response (number of responders and response lag)

Action Characteristic	*Information Content*	*Competitive Response*
Magnitude of Action		
Strategic (large magnitude)	Difficult to interpret, unfamiliar, and uncertain information	Few responders; slow
Tactical (small magnitude)	Easier to interpret, more familiar, and certain information	Many responders; fast
Scope of Action		
Wide (affects many rivals)	More information, greater information leakage	Many responders; fast
Narrow (affects few rivals)	Less information, less information leakage	Few responders; slow
Threat of Action		
Major (steal many customers)	More communication from customers about the action and greater information leakage	Many responders; fast
Minor (steal fewer customers)	Less communication from customers about the action and less information leakage	Few responders; slow
Radicality of Action		
Radical	Unfamiliar information; cannot use past experiences	Few responders; slow
Not Radical	Familiar information; can use past experiences	Many responders; fast
Implementation Requirements of Action		
Difficult to Implement	Communication breakdowns and overload	Few responders; slow
Easy to Implement	Smooth flow of communication	Many responders; fast

these characteristics are theorized to represent, and the predictions regarding number of responders and response lag.

Measures

In this section there is a description of the measures used in the four studies. This description parallels that in the previous section.

Magnitude of Action: Strategic Versus Tactical. Magnitude of action was defined as "strategic" or "tactical." Six strategic management professors categorized the different actions from each study as strategic or tactical, based on the extent of resources devoted to each action. There was very high agreement among the judges in the classification of these actions into the two categories—in fact, only one incidence of disagreement. The number of strategic versus tactical actions in each study was as follows.

	Strategic	*Tactical*	*Total*
Airlines	33	123	156
Electrical Manufacturing	18	4	22
High Technology	11	14	25
Computer Retailing	23	4	27

Scope of Action. This variable reflects the breadth of an action or the total number of competitors affected by it. Competitors affected by an action were defined as those firms that provided a product and/or service in at least one of the markets affected by the action. The scope was determined by counting the total number of companies serving the markets affected by the action. For instance, if an action affected 5 markets served by 10 competitors, the scope of the action would be 10. This measure is available only for the airline study.

Threat of Action. This variable was measured in two different ways, the first being an objective measure, the second a perceptual one. In the airline study, threat of action was measured as the extent to which an action affected a given competitor's key markets. That is, the proportion of a competitor's total number of customers affected by an action was actually measured. For example, if an airline served 50,000 customers from an airport affected by an action, and served a total of 500,000 customers at all its airports (the remaining 450,000 customers were unaffected by the action), then the threat measure would be .10 (50,000 affected by an action divided by 500,000 total customers). This measure varies with each event since different markets and competitors were affected in each event. An average threat score was used to test the hypothesis relating the degree of threat and the number of responders.

In the electrical manufacturing study, managers were asked to respond to three questions about the characteristics of an action to which their firm had responded. These three questions focused on the extent to which the action was perceived as visible, threatening, and damaging to third-party (customers or suppliers) relations. The scale was labeled *Threat of Action* and was computed by summing the standardized scores to each question ($\alpha = 0.74$).

Radicality. Radicality is the extent to which an action was perceived as departing from the basic competitive norms and operating assumptions of the industry. Managers were asked to respond to three questions about the extent to which an action was radical and the extent to which the action resulted in an opportunity for the competitor. The scale was labeled Radicality and was computed by summing the standardized scores to each question ($\alpha = 0.85$). This measure is available only for the electrical manufacturing study.

Action Implementation Requirement. The degree of time spent in implementing an action is defined as the action's implementation requirement. The measure was determined by the time difference between the date on which the action was reported and the date on which it was actually implemented. For example, if the action was reported on December 1 but did not take effect until January 1, the action implementation requirement would be 31 days. This measure is available only for the airline study.

Consistent with the definitions provided in Chapter 2, *response lag* was measured by the amount of time it took a firm to respond to a competitor's action. The amount of time was measured by the temporal difference between the date on which a specific competitive action was first reported and when the response occurred. *Number of responders* was measured as the aggregate number of responders by all rivals to a given competitive action, yielding a measure of the number of responses to each competitive action. This second response measure is available only for the airline study.

Data Analysis and Findings

In this section we describe only the results obtained through the formal testing of hypotheses. It was possible to formally test the hypotheses in the airline study and the electrical manufacturing study. A subsequent section will integrate these findings with evidence from the other studies.

Airline Study

A separate regression model was run with response lag and number of responders as dependent variables. Overall examination of Table 4.2 yields strong support for the hypothesis that a competitive response is, at least in part, a function of characteristics of the action.

The first model regressed response lag against the four characteristics of action. Overall, speed of competitive response is a function of the magnitude of the action, its scope, the threat of the action, and its implementation requirements. More specifically and as hypothesized, as the magnitude of competitive actions increase, response time increases ($\beta = .539$; $p<.001$); as the implementation requirements of the action increase, response

Table 4.2 Regression Analysis of Action Characteristics on Response Characteristics in the Airline Industry

	Number of Responses[a]	*Response Lag*[b]
Magnitude of Action (strategic)	–.1165*	.5386***
	(.1029)	(2.2512)
Scope of Action	–.1215*	.1270**
	(.0081)	(.1337)
Threat of Action	.7754*	–.0808+
	(.0013)	(.0756)
Implementation Requirements of Action	–.0931+	.1777***
	(.0014)	(.0266)
R^2	.59	.39
F-Test	62.88***	60.13***

+*p*<.10
**p*<.05
***p*<.01
****p*<.001
[a] *n* = 161
[b] *n* = 364

time increases (β = .177; *p*<.001); and as the threat of the action increases, response time decreases (β = -.080; *p*<.05). Contrary to expectations, as the scope of an action increases, response time increases (β = .127; *p*<.01).

The second model regressed number of responders against the four action characteristics. As with the case of response lag described above, the number of responders to an action is, at least in part, a function of the characteristics of action. Namely, as the magnitude of action increases, the number of responders to the action decreases (β = -.117; *p*<.05); as the implementation requirements of the action increase, the number of responders to the action decreases (β = -.093; *p*<.05); and as the threat of the action increases, the number of responders increases (β = .775; *p*<.001). Contrary to expectations, as the scope of the action increases, the number of responders decreases (β = .121; *p*<.05).

Overall, the four characteristics of response account for 40% of the variation in response lag (*F* = 60.136; *p*<.001) and 60% of

Table 4.3 Regression Analysis of Action Characteristics on Response Time in the Electrical Manufacturing Study ($n = 22$)

	Standardized β	*t-value*
Threat of Action	–.4043	–2.95***
Radicality of Action	–.4074	–2.97***
External Orientation[a]	–.3466	–2.40**
Formalization[a]	.0233	.87
R^2	.56	
F-Test	10.199***	

[a] External orientation and structural complexity will be discussed in Chapter 5.
**$p<.05$
***$p<.01$

the variation in the number of responders ($F = 62.88$; $p<.001$). Now let us consider the results from the electrical manufacturing study.

Electrical Manufacturing Study

Table 4.3 reports the regression results between the composite measures of the threat of action, its radicality, and response lag. As in the airline study, actions that are threatening are associated with faster response times ($\beta = -40$; $p<.01$). In addition, actions that are more radical, or actions that defy industry norms of behavior, are associated with longer response times ($\beta = -41$; $p<.01$).

Integration and Descriptive Results

Overall, the results of formal testing of the hypotheses suggest that the underlying characteristics of an action can be important predictors of competitive response. In this section of the chapter we will discuss and augment the results with descriptive evidence gathered from interviews with executives.

Consider first the influence of the magnitude of action on response. Table 4.4 reports the relationship between the magnitude

Table 4.4 Magnitude of Action and Response Time

	Type of Industry			
Magnitude of Action	*High Tech*	*High Tech*	*Computer Retailing*	*Domestic Airlines*
Strategic	271 days	540 days	47 days	34 days 1.15 responses
Tactical	124 days	165 days	24 days	8 days 2.40 responses

of the action and response lag for each of the four studies. As suggested above, response times to strategic actions are significantly greater than those to tactical actions. In fact, on average, the response times to strategic actions are almost three times greater than to tactical actions (the range is from 1.95 times in the high technology study to 4.25 times in the computer retailing study). It is significant that in all four studies the same relationship was found. The information contained in actions of major magnitude is probably much more difficult for rivals to interpret, understand, and manage. Thus it seems safe to conclude that, in general, firms respond more slowly to actions of greater magnitude than to those of lesser magnitude. Actions of lesser magnitude, then, may not yield a sustainable competitive advantage simply because of the rapidity of response. In addition, in the airline industry, more than twice as many competitors respond to lower magnitude tactical actions (M = 2.40) than to strategic actions (M = 1.15). This variable was measured only in the airline study.

Regarding the relationship between the threat of the action and response, the results are consistent in both the airline study and the electrical manufacturing study: As the threat of action increases (the action directly threatens to steal a higher proportion of a rival's customers), response times decrease. Thus, actions that directly target the customers of rivals, and thus threaten them, tend to increase the flow of competitor information, accelerating the speed of rival responses. In addition, as found in the airline study, the threat of an action is positively related to the number of responders. Directly targeting a competitor, then, probably raises or intensifies competition, potentially creating an unprofitable situation for all. This result is suggested by Porter (1980) and is consistent with the perspective of Dutton and Jackson (1987), who argued that managers would be more likely to respond to actions that directly threaten them. Finally, the importance of minimizing the extent to which an action is threatening is consistent with the market signaling literature (Porter, 1980), which posits that firms should announce or package their competitive movements to minimize provocation.

The implementation requirements of an action also influence response in the airline industry. Thus, designing actions that are difficult to implement might work to create an important barrier to response. Not surprisingly, as the magnitude of an action increases, so does its implementation difficulty.

Concerning the scope of the action, the results from the airline study contradict the hypothesis. That is, actions of wide scope tend to decrease the total level of rivalry, both slowing the speed of rival responses and lowering the number of responders. Our interpretation of this contrary finding is that rival firms will not perceive an action as threatening if it does not directly target them. That is, when an action is targeted at only one or two rivals, the motives and goals behind the action will be easier to understand and will be perceived as more threatening by rivals, precipitating a fast response only by those firms that are directly affected.

Regarding the radicality of actions, we found that actions that tend to defy industry norms of behavior are associated with longer response times. This finding supports Porter's (1980) notion that moves which cannot be matched because they violate a competitor's beliefs and assumptions are ideal moves for firms to make. Competitors will be unfamiliar with the information available on radical moves, thus providing one explanation for the delay in their response.

Formal tests of the hypotheses discussed above indicate that the relationship between characteristics of action and response is relatively straightforward, but evidence from case studies suggests greater complexity. Take, for example, the relationship between the magnitude of action and the threat of action in the computer retailing industry. We have already reported that in the computer retailing industry, responses to actions of lower magnitude were significantly faster than responses to actions of greater magnitude. Interestingly, this quick response occurs despite the fact that executives label such low magnitude actions as *less* threatening. In fact, in the computer retailing study, 73% of all responses were to actions that were considered to be of low threat. Also of importance, the vast majority of the low threat, low magnitude actions were price actions to which these retailers must be sensitive, even if they are not perceived as critically threatening. This finding, although anecdotal, suggests that actions of less magnitude, which require fewer resources and can be reversed, often elicit responses automatically, perhaps just so that the responding firm can stay competitive.

Firms responded to actions of greater magnitude more slowly, despite perceiving them as more threatening. It is perhaps in this context that the importance of resource requirements of strategic actions of greater magnitude can best be understood. That is, despite recognizing the need to respond to high threat actions, the firm faces the difficulty of gathering the necessary resources to respond; the difficulty in gathering these resources probably acts as a barrier, thus slowing down the speed of rivals' responses.

Computer retailing firms which responded to a competitor's action report that the reason for doing so is to protect their short-term business performance, rather than to achieve any particular strategic goal. Most often, the specific reason for a response was to protect sales volume. Very few firms reported a response that was based on the long-term goal or strategy of their business. In spite of the widely held perceptions that the personal computer market was growing rapidly at the time this study took place, most firms reported being in a defensive and protective mode.

Table 4.5 Initial Moves With Associated Responses and Response Times in the High-Technology Study

Type of Move	*Number of Firms*	*%*	*Response Time (in months)*
Cutting price	12	48	6.17
Introducing new product	11	44	18.18
Advertising	2	8	1.50
	25	100	

Type of Response	*Number of Firms*	*%*	*Response Time (in months)*
Cutting price	9	36	7.11
Advertising	6	24	7.50
Introducing new product	4	16	22.60
Altering R&D	2	8	10.00
Improving product quality	4	16	8.75
	25	100	

Still, most of the competitive actions in this industry to which firms responded were price moves. In fact, price moves were the most frequent (62%), and these were almost always imitated. Other popular actions evoking responses included promotion campaigns (21%) and new product introduction moves (17%).

The response times to pricing actions were incredibly fast, averaging 7 days, whereas the response times to new promotional actions were slower, averaging 31 days. Consistent with the results reported above on the magnitude of actions, response times to new product introductions were, on average, more than 47 days.

The complexity of the relationship between competitive actions and response is further demonstrated in an analysis of the specific moves and responses in the high-technology study. Table 4.5 reports the different kinds of actions that were identified. The most frequent competitive move by these firms was price-cutting, constituting 48% of the initial moves. New product introductions were also popular, accounting for 44% of the moves. The third type of move was advertising/promotion, which accounted for 8% of the initial actions.

Table 4.5 also identifies the different responses to these moves. As in the case of initial actions, the most frequent response was price-cutting, which accounted for 36% of the responses. Advertising, which involved 24% of the responses, was second in frequency. Introducing new products and improving quality tied as the third most frequent response; each accounted for 16%. Finally, 8% of the responses involved altering research and development efforts.

There are important differences in the timing of responses to the different moves. Most important, and as already noted, lower magnitude actions elicited faster responses than those of greater magnitude. For example, firms responded to minor moves involving advertising most quickly, averaging 1.5 months. Similarly, firms responded to price-cutting moves in 6.17 months. The longer response time for price cuts vis-à-vis advertising may be due to the difficulty of learning about changes in competitor pricing in this somewhat fragmented industry, where many products are sold at the wholesale level and price information is often closely guarded. Not surprisingly, the strategic move of new product introductions had the longest response time (18.18 months).

Table 4.5 also reports the times associated with implementing alternative responses. For instance, price-cutting and advertising responses were implemented relatively quickly, averaging around 7 months. This relationship is to be expected since these two types of responses are relatively minor in nature. Altering research and development and improving product quality, on the other hand, took longer to implement, averaging 9 and 10 months, respectively. Finally, responding with new product introductions took the most time, averaging more than 22 months. Thus the delay in implementing a response appears to be proportional to the magnitude of the response.

There was much greater variety in the different actions identified in the airline study. Table 4.6 lists these actions and their frequency. Although the great number of different actions

Table 4.6 Actions in the Airline Industry

	Actions	*Responses*
1. Intra-industry merger and acquisition	2(1.0%)	2(0.5%)
2. Changes in ticket purchase requirements	6(3.1%)	14(3.3%)
3. Promotion	15(7.9%)	29(6.9%)
4. Market expansion	16(8.4%)	17(4.1%)
5. Special introductory fares	15(7.9%)	2(0.5%)
6. Changes in organizational structure	1(0.5%)	2(0.5%)
7. Price increase	20(10.4%)	58(13.9%)
8. Changes in fare plan or structure	11(5.8%)	53(12.7%)
9. Introduction of a new kind of plane	2(1.0%)	2(0.5%)
10. Joint promotion with distributors	9(4.7%)	34(8.1%)
11. Vertical integration with feeders	3(1.6%)	3(0.7%)
12. Joint promotion with other firms	2(1.0%)	5(1.2%)
13. Market withdrawal	7(3.7%)	3(0.7%)
14. Service improvement	5(2.6%)	4(0.9%)
15. Introduction of "Frequent Flyer" program	2(1.0%)	5(1.2%)
16. Price cut	75(39.3%)	185(44.4%)
Total	191(100%)	418(100%)

identified in the airline industry (16) suggests greater competitive complexity, a closer examination reveals significant symmetry or overlap with the actions identified in the other studies. For example, 64% of the actions and 74% of the responses involve pricing actions of one sort or another (fare structure changes, price increases, price decreases, and so on). Moreover, 15% of the actions and 18% of the responses were promotional campaigns of one type or another (including new advertising campaigns and miscellaneous joint promotions). Finally, 16% of the actions and 8% of the responses involved actions of greater magnitude (e.g., mergers, acquisitions, vertical integration, and new product introductions). Thus, there are more similarities than differences between the types of actions across the different studies.

As in the other studies, the response times and number of responders varied across these three broad groups of actions. For example, the response times to pricing and promotional actions were 7 days and 15 days, respectively. As already reported, the response time to actions of high magnitude was 34 days.

Research Questions

We can now turn our attention to future research questions. This chapter examined the relationship between action characteristics and rivalry. In each of the studies reported, there was support for the general hypothesis that the characteristics of action undertaken by a firm influence the manner in which rival firms react. Indeed, many competitors respond swiftly to low magnitude, wide scope actions that are threatening. In contrast, actions of major magnitude, characterized by narrow scope and lower threat, provoke fewer and slower responses.

Regarding type of action, it is important to note that the different types identified in each study herein are reasonably consistent with one another. Each study identified pricing actions, promotional actions, and actions of greater magnitude, such as new product introductions. Moreover, these categories fit reasonably well into the three general research areas identified in the beginning of this chapter: pricing, advertising/promotion, and new patented product introductions. Such consistency suggests that current research has been accurate in identifying key strategic actions for investigation and highlighting the basic strategic alternatives available to managers.

Although the results of this chapter are significant in shedding light on the relationship between competitive actions and rivalry, future research possibilities are numerous and include: (a) the identification of relationships between the different action characteristics; (b) the exploration of additional characteristics of action; and (c) additional fieldwork to determine what variables or dimensions of action are perceived as most important by managers. Table 4.7 summarizes these and other possibilities; each will be discussed in turn.

Table 4.7 Future Research Questions on Competitive Actions and Rivalry

1. What is the relationship between different characteristics of action?
1a. What is the relationship between an action's magnitude, threat, scope, and radicality?
1b. What is the relationship between action magnitude and action implementation requirements?
2. What is the most appropriate measure of action implementation requirements?
3. What is the most appropriate continuous measure of action magnitude?
4. How do the threat, scope, and radicality of a patented product action combine to influence rivalry?
5. In what ways can the variety of actions that occur in an industry be combined to best explain rivalry?
6. What is the relationship between rivalry and the level of:
   - innovativeness of an action?
   - risk involved in an action?
   - complexity of an action?
   - secrecy in an action?
7. What are the key characteristics of secret actions?
8. To what extent do managers actually access the information in a rival's action?
9. To what extent do actions stimulate response in the absence of other strategic variables (e.g., the reputation of the actors or the industry context)?

Given the likely correlation between different characteristics of action (e.g., that high threat actions would also be of narrow scope), an important question concerns identifying the characteristics of action that are most crucial for explaining rivalry. For the current research, action magnitude seems more important than whether the action was perceived as threatening. For example, firms in the computer-retailing study responded very quickly to actions that are easier to imitate, despite their being labeled as non-threatening. Moreover, there was no relationship between the scope of an action and its magnitude, in spite of the fact that minor actions (e.g., price) would likely have greater scope. These are perplexing findings that can be clarified only by further research.

Indeed, one important area of future research concerns the concept of action implementation requirements. More specifically, an important issue is the relationship between the magnitude of an action and its implementation difficulty. For example, is there a one-to-one relationship? It is one thing to announce an action and quite another to implement it. While this research emphasized the time taken to implement an action, other possible implementation indicators include the number of personnel required to implement the action, the number of distribution outlets through which the product must be implemented, and the experience of the firm in carrying out actions of a similar nature.

As noted, a significant amount of past research has been devoted to the ease with which rivals can duplicate patented new product introductions. Concerning the duplication of patented products, it would be possible to examine how different characteristics of action, such as magnitude, threat, scope, and radicality, work together to influence the ease of imitation of patented products.

Future research should identify additional characteristics and measures of competitive actions. A starting point would be to identify a continuous measure of action magnitude, building on the dichotomous measure employed here. Possible measures include the dollar cost of the action, the number of personnel devoted to formulating and implementing the action, and the expected gain or outcome from it.

Another potentially important variable for examination would be the extent to which an action is innovative. Although this research emphasized the extent of radicality, innovation is different in that it concerns the level of creativity in an action. Research on advertising has concluded that it is the extent of innovation in the promotional material, as opposed to the amount of ad exposure, which creates an advantage for firms. Thus, innovation is not limited to new products but can relate to a wide variety of actions, including pricing. For example, the aggressive pricing actions of People Express were extremely innovative, revolutionizing pricing in the airline industry.

Three other action characteristics of potential interest are the degree of action risk, the extent of action complexity, and the level of action secrecy. Concerning the degree of action risk, competitive responses could be expected to vary when the action involves significant commitments of scarce resources, which, once committed, are difficult to reverse. Some potential measures of risk include both the expected return on investment from the action and the subjective ratings of the action's riskiness.

In addition, rivals may have a difficult time responding to actions that require complex combinations of human and physical resources to carry out. For example, a new product introduction, based on scientific research from a special research lab employing hundreds of scientists and market-tested with a sales force of thousands, would generally be more difficult for rivals to duplicate than the action of a sole entrepreneur. One potential measure of complexity is the number of different kinds of resources required to formulate and implement the action. Finally, one would expect no response to actions that have been secretly undertaken. Indeed, secrecy is a crucial yet under- researched area of competition. Case studies would be required to examine the effectiveness of clandestine actions and to learn more about their key characteristics.

Finally, as in the case of the indicators of reputation discussed in the previous chapter, the question exists as to the extent to which managers actually access the information in a rival's action, or for that matter, whether a rival's actions are the primary stimulus to a response. Thus, future research to determine the relationship between direct assessment of actions and rivalry is needed to more precisely predict the effects of action characteristics on competition.

5

Responders and Rivalry

THE extent to which a firm's actions result in a competitive advantage and improved performance depends largely on the responses of rivals. For example, competitors virtually ignored Timex's unconventional move into the U.S. watch market with

---

AUTHORS' NOTE: Portions of this chapter were adapted from: (a) "Organizational Information Processing: Competitive Responses and Performance in the U.S. Domestic Airline Industry" by K. G. Smith, C. Grimm, M. Gannon, and M. J. Chen, 1991, *Academy of Management Journal, 34*, pp. 60-85. Copyright 1991 by the Academy of Management. Adapted by permission. (b) "Predictors of Response Time to Competitive Strategic Actions: Preliminary Theory and Evidence" by K. G. Smith, C. Grimm, M. J. Chen, and M. Gannon, 1989, *Journal of Business Research, 18*, pp. 245-258. Copyright 1989 by Elsevier Science Publishing Company. Adapted by permission. (c) "Competitive Moves and Responses Among High-Technology Firms" by K. G. Smith, M.Gannon, and C. Grimm, in H. Glass (Ed.), *The Handbook of Strategy* (ch. 31, p. 1), 1990, New York: Warren, Gorham & Lamont. Copyright 1989 by Warren, Gorham & Lamont, Inc. Adapted by permission.

a line of low-priced watches after World War II. During the 13 years when competitors did not respond, Timex enjoyed superior profits. In contrast, Maxwell House mounted a quick and aggressive response to Procter and Gamble's entry into the retail coffee business. This fast response forced Procter and Gamble to rethink its entry decision. These examples, which were briefly discussed in Chapter 1, serve to remind the reader of the importance of competitive responses, or lack thereof, to the overall effectiveness of actions. In short, firms want to take actions against competitors who have a low probability of responding and react very slowly.[1]

Understanding and predicting the likely responses of rivals is the primary focus of competitor analysis (Porter, 1980). The idea is that firms can predict a rival's future actions and reactions by carefully studying them. Porter (1985) argues that there is a distinct advantage to a firm that understands the future behavior of its rivals: "A principle that emerges is that there is a high payout to anticipating which firms represent the most likely challengers and what their logical avenues of attack might be" (p. 487). With adequate information regarding the plausible responses of rivals, firms can more effectively design their actions to impede response.

The emphasis of this chapter is on competitor analysis, specifically the identification of factors that will empirically predict a rival's response. The chapter employs information-processing theory to address questions such as which firms will be likely responders to an action, which rivals are likely to imitate an action, which ones will respond quickly or slowly, and what will be the order of response among a group of rivals. A central argument of the chapter is that a firm's response decision is a function of both the competitive information it possesses and how this information flows throughout the organization (Knight & McDaniel, 1979; Mortensen, 1972).

Figure 5.1 links the organizational information-processing emphasis of this chapter to the overall communication model presented in Chapter 1. First, we develop an organizational information-processing model with three central dimensions: information sensing, information analyzing, and information selection and

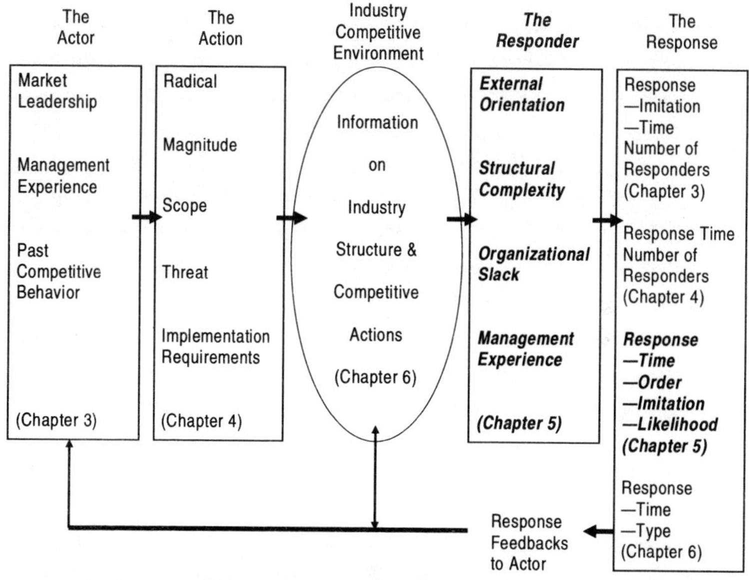

Figure 5.1. The Focus of Chapter 5

retention. Next, these three dimensions are used to predict different characteristics of response, namely: response imitation, response likelihood, response time, and response order.[2] Finally, we test these predictions, using the data sets described in Chapter 2.

An Information-Processing Perspective on Competitor Analysis

Different firms will view information on actors and their actions in disparate ways. That is, they may obtain information on a competitor's action through diverse channels, may process and transmit this information according to different procedures and practices, and may interpret the information in distinct ways. In the communication literature this is referred to as "decoding the message" (Berlo, 1960). How firms decode information on competitors and their actions depends on their information-processing systems and capacities (Huber & Daft, 1987; March & Simon, 1958).

Conceptually, organizational information-processing includes the transfer and analysis of sensory data from the boundary of the organization to the key decision makers, and the selection of and emphasis on this information in their decision making (Huber & Daft, 1987; Knight & Mc Daniel, 1979). The organizational information-processing model is identified in Figure 5.2 and involves three related dimensions: information sensory systems, information-processing and analyzing mechanisms, and information selection and retention.

Organizational members must first sense or perceive information about a competitor's action in order for a response to occur. This is problematic since competitors have an incentive to conceal, bluff, or obfuscate the significance of their actions. Hewes, Graham, Doelger, and Pavitt (1985, p. 299) describe the problem in the following manner: "Interpreting messages is a dirty business. From the simplest greetings to the most complex rationalization, messages are inherently ambiguous and sometimes intentionally misleading." Similarly, Porter (1980) notes that recognizing and accurately reading market actions is a major part of the strategic management process. Consequently, the sensing systems that organizations employ to assess competitors' actions are of critical importance (Huber & Daft, 1987).

Even if an organization has extensive sensing capacity, it may fail to react if it cannot transfer the information from the boundary of the organization to decision makers and back to response implementors (Huber & Ullman, 1973). For example, a field salesperson may learn about a competitor's move from a customer (the perception step), after which he or she informs the area sales manager, who may modify, delay, or block the transmission of this information to the next level of the organization. Even if the information finally reaches the decision maker, it may be too distorted to be useful. Therefore, the information capacity and analyzing mechanisms of an organization will also affect its responses.

Although the firm's information capacity and analyzing mechanisms will affect the way information is processed, the selection and retention of information by decision makers is impor-

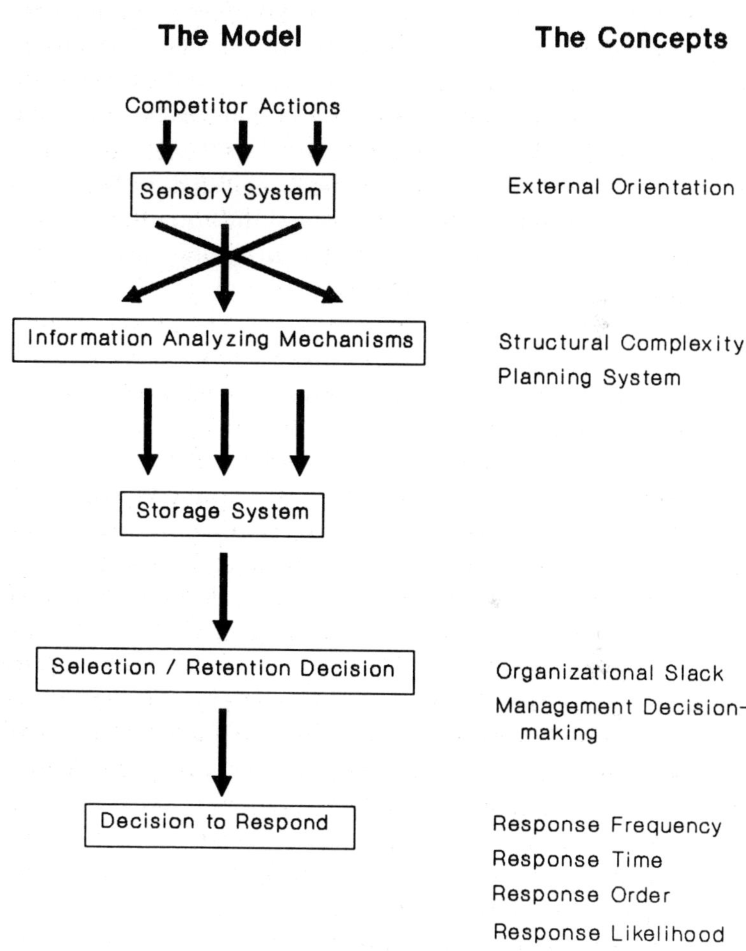

Figure 5.2. An Organization Information-Processing Model and Key Concepts

tant as well (Cohen, 1958; Downs, 1966; O'Reilly & Roberts, 1974). Information on a rival's action can create a significant amount of uncertainty for a firm's decision makers, who engage in search activities in order to reduce this uncertainty (March

& Simon, 1958). Human factors will especially influence search procedures. For example, experienced managers may select and retain information based entirely on their past encounters with rivals, whereas managers without such experience may conduct a much more thorough information search. Thus, the manner in which decision makers select and retain information can also be utilized to predict response.

The three information-processing dimensions described above are consistent with Porter's (1980) conceptual model of competitor analysis, where rivals can be understood by their strategies, capabilities, goals, and assumptions. For example, a rival pursuing a product differentiation strategy, perhaps attempting to build brand loyalty, would require a greater ability to sense changing customer needs than would a rival pursuing a more internally oriented low-cost strategy. Moreover, analyzing and processing competitive information is an important capability of a firm that can greatly determine the adroitness of its response. Finally, the goals and assumptions of rivals can be directly inferred by the way decision makers select and retain certain kinds of information and how their biases affect these processes. In this regard, Porter (1980) describes how the goals and assumptions of managers can be inferred from their backgrounds.

In the next section of this chapter we link the three information-processing dimensions to different characteristics of response. The characteristics of response, which we have described in detail in Chapter 2 include: response imitation, response likelihood, response time, and response order.

Organizational Information-Processing and Competitive Response

Information Sensory Systems

A response cannot occur if a firm or decision maker does not realize that a competitor has made a move. Organizations vary significantly in their ability to sense environmental changes.

For example, Miles and Snow (1978) characterize defenders as "internals," with a primary orientation toward efficiency and internal operations. In contrast, they describe prospectors as "externals," with a greater orientation toward environmental openness and change; such firms will be characterized by an emphasis on marketing and customer relations (Miles & Snow, 1978) and they will have proportionately more boundary-spanning activities (Adams, 1976). We predict that a firm's external orientation will be positively related to likelihood of response, and negatively related to propensity to imitate, response time, and response order. That is, as a rival's external orientation increases, the probability that it will respond to a move will also increase. Moreover, if a response were to occur in a firm with an external orientation, it would likely be fast, early, and non-imitative.

The logic for these predictions is that firms with external orientations will be more likely to sense a rival's actions. In addition, firms with an external orientation will be more capable of implementing competitive responses. For instance, firms with extensive marketing and customer relations personnel will be in a better position to carry out a price cut or new product introduction than will firms with fewer of these personnel. Firms with a less external orientation (and thus perhaps a more internal orientation) will not be as capable of sensing relevant information in their environments, and they will be less capable of implementing an external response (Pearce, 1983; Pfeffer, 1972). Accordingly, one would expect that, as a firm's external orientation increases, it will more likely respond and, on average, respond more swiftly and earlier than rivals.

Firms with external orientations will not only acquire information sooner, but they will also be more capable of gathering a richer array of information (Aldrich, 1979). Information richness is defined as the information-carrying capacity of data; some data are extremely informative while other data provide little, if any, information (Daft & Lengel, 1984). Externally oriented firms, with a richer array of competitor information than internally oriented firms, will be more capable of developing, analyzing, and evaluating response options. In contrast, internally oriented firms, in the absence of additional information-gathering, will have a poorer or less rich information base to use when deciding whether to respond. Information with a low degree of carrying capacity provides fewer opportunities for understanding and meaning (Huber & Daft, 1987). Daft and Lengel (1984) describe how low information richness can lead to oversimplification and the "mindless reduction of unequivocality" (p. 212). Therefore, internally oriented firms will be more likely to follow and imitate the actions of rivals than will externally oriented firms.

Information-Processing and Analyzing Mechanisms

An organization's structure largely determines its information capacity and analyzing mechanisms (Galbraith, 1977; Huber & Daft, 1987). Structure can vary in many ways, but one critical element affecting the flow of competitive information is structural complexity (Miles, 1980; Zey-Ferrell, 1979). It refers specifically to the number of levels through which the information must pass between the boundary spanner and decision makers, and the formality of the procedures designed to manage this information (Miles; Zey-Ferrell). As structural complexity increases, so too do the chances that the information being communicated will be distorted, repackaged, or blocked (Brenner & Sigband, 1973; Conrath, 1967).

Structurally complex organizations will have difficulty analyzing and transferring the information from the boundary spanners in the external environment to decision makers and then back to response implementors. Accordingly, structural complexity and formalization will be negatively related to likelihood of response, and positively related to propensity to imitate, average response lag, and average response order. In other words, as structural complexity increases, the probability of response will decrease. Further, if a response were to occur in a structurally complex organization, it would probably be slow, late, and imitative.

Numerous studies have shown that as structural complexity increases, so too does the probability that the information being transmitted will be distorted and/or totally blocked (e.g., Aldrich, 1979; Galbraith, 1977; Rousseau, 1978). Information from decision makers to implementors may be similarly blocked by increased structural complexity. Thus, decision makers in structurally complex firms will: (a) receive competitor information late; and (b) receive less rich competitor information on which to develop response alternatives. Hence, decision makers will have greater difficulty responding and will, on average, respond slower and later than decision makers in less structurally complex firms. With less rich information, decision makers will tend to oversimplify and prematurely close off options. Such firms will be more likely to follow and imitate the actions of rivals than will less structurally complex firms.

Information Selection and Retention

No matter how effectively the information system is structured, decision makers must harness the information provided and make meaningful interpretations of it before responding. Most important, they need to evaluate the intention and potential consequences of each competitor's action, and these are, at least initially, frequently uncertain or unknown (Barney, 1986; Nelson & Winter, 1982). This uncertainty creates problems for decision makers, which they attempt to reduce to controllable levels (Duncan, 1972; Galbraith, 1977). Thus, decision makers engage in information-search activities to reduce or eliminate uncertainty (March & Simon, 1958). Information search can be influenced by both the costs of search and the human characteristics of decision makers. These will be considered in turn.

In terms of resources, March and Simon emphasize that information search is costly. Thus, organizational resources and capabilities have the potential to influence the speed and exhaustiveness of the decision makers' information-search process. In this regard, organizational slack is a concept directly related to a firm's resources and capabilities. Bourgeois (1981) defines slack as: "that cushion of actual or potential resources which allows an organization to adapt successfully to internal pressures for adjustment or to external pressures for change in policy as well as to initiate changes in strategy with respect to the external environment" (p. 30). In general, we predict that the degree of slack resources is positively related to likelihood of response, and negatively related to propensity to imitate, average response lag, and average response order. Alternatively, as slack resources in an organization increase, so does the probability of a response. Additionally, responses from a firm with high levels of slack resources are likely to be fast, early, and non-imitative.

Cyert and March (1963) note that slack resources enhance an organization's adaptability. Thompson (1967) contends that slack protects the firm from its environment, and Chakravarthy (1982) points out that strategic choices are constrained when resources are low. Meyer (1982) found that organizations with slack resources respond faster and in a more effective manner to environmental crisis than do organizations with limited resources. Moreover, organizations with slack resources can afford sophisticated search activities, such as an integrated computer information system, to enhance their search process. Further, firms with ample slack resources will be better able to implement a response. For example, such firms may instantly order overtime hours to hasten the implementation process. Conversely, firms without these resources may have to take the time to develop a resource base to finance their response. Lieberman and Montgomery (1988) have argued that to mimic a rival's action is generally less costly than to undertake an entirely new action; that is, the firm benefits from the free rider effect. Therefore, firms with fewer slack resources will be more likely, on average, to imitate rivals' actions than will firms with greater slack resources.

Finally, human factors can bias the information-search process (Cohen, 1958; Downs, 1966; March & Simon, 1958; O'Reilly & Roberts, 1974). In particular, the education and experience levels of the top management team can critically influence information search activities of the organization and thus decision making (Hambrick & Mason, 1984). In general, we predict that lower levels of experience but higher levels of education among top-level teams are positively related to likelihood of response, and negatively related to propensity to imitate, average response lag, and average response order. That is, firms managed by less experienced but higher educated teams will be more likely to respond. Moreover, if a response were to occur in an organization with a less experienced but better educated management team, such responses would be fast, early, and non-imitative.

Education and experience levels relate to a manager's knowledge and skill base (Hambrick & Mason, 1984). For example, more educated managers will be more exhaustive in information-search activities, and this emphasis results in greater information richness from which to make a response decision (Hambrick & Mason). They will also be more aware of the importance of competing aggressively in the marketplace; they will more likely have mechanisms in place for processing competitive information. Consequently, one would expect educated managers to be more likely to respond and to do so, on average, faster and earlier than less educated managers. Moreover, because educated managers will have a richer array of information leading to a greater variety of response options, they will be less likely to imitate the actions of rivals.

More experienced managers, on the other hand, will tend to employ less exhaustive search procedures, often simply utilizing processes and responses that have worked well in the past (Carson, 1972). According to Hambrick and Mason, managers retain their cognitive and emotional experiences throughout their careers. Managers with many years of experience in a single industry will thus have a limited knowledge and skill base from which to make response decisions and will be more likely to engage in "limited search" (Cyert & March, 1963) when faced with a competitive action. Carson asserted that experienced managers will tend to avoid risky actions. They will more likely develop explicit and well-defined cognitive models, and that can affect their flexibility (Hitt & Barr, 1989). In contrast, less experienced managers will tend to engage in more novel and risky actions. They will have more stamina and be better able to learn new behaviors (Child, 1974). Therefore, one would expect less experienced managers to be more aggressive, making them more likely to respond. Furthermore, less experienced managers will, on average, respond faster and earlier than more experienced managers.[3] Because they will tend to be risk-takers, less experienced managers will also be more likely not to mimic the actions of rivals.

Table 5.1 summarizes the different information-processing dimensions, the information content they reflect, and their link to the four characteristics of response. In the next section we discuss some key measurement issues and more specifically define the measures used in each study.

Measures

In this section there is a description of the measures used to test the various hypotheses. It was possible to formally test the hypotheses in the airline study and the electrical manufacturing study.

Airline Study

The various predictions in the airline study are tested with average organizational response measures for each of the response attributes. In other words, the unit of observation is a firm's responses over a given year.[4] Thus, a pooled cross-section/time series data set was constructed containing 104 observations for each of the response characteristics. These 104 observations are based on the responses of 23 different airlines.

Response likelihood was calculated by summing the number of times a firm responded to competitors' actions during a given year and dividing this figure by the number of times the firm had an opportunity to respond. Consequently, firms that score

Table 5.1 Summary of Information-Processing Dimension, the Informational Content They Reflect, and the Response Predictions

Information Dimension	*Information Content*	*Competitive Response*
Information Sensory Systems		
External Orientation	more, faster, and richer information	likely, non-imitative, fast, and early response
Internal Orientation	less, slow, and less rich information	less likely, imitative, slow, and late response
Information-Processing and Analyzing Mechanisms		
Structurally Simple	more, faster, and richer information	likely, non-imitative, and early response
Structurally Complex	less and slow information; information overload and distortion	less likely, imitative, slow, and late response
Information Selection and Retention		
High Levels of Slack	high search capacity; more, faster, and richer information	likely, non-imitative, fast, and early response
Low Levels of Slack	low search capacity; less and slow information; information overload	less likely, imitative, slow, and late response
Less Experienced but More Educated Managers	high search capacity; more, faster, and richer information	likely, non-imitative, fast, and early response
More Experienced but Less Educated Managers	low search capacity; less and slow information; information overload	less likely, imitative, slow, and late response

high on this scale are more likely responders. The number of times the firm had an opportunity to respond was obtained by counting the number of actions that potentially affected a focal airline (there was no double counting).

Response imitation, or the degree to which a response imitated an action, was measured in terms of the concurrence of the action type and the response type. An imitation score was created to measure the degree of duplication involved in each response. The imitation score was calculated so that when the type of response was the same as the type of action (for example, a price cut in response to a price cut), the imitation score equaled 1; when the response type was not the same as the action type (for example, a price cut in response to a new product introduction), the imitation score equaled 0.

Response lag was measured by the amount of time it took a firm to respond to a competitor's action. The amount of time was measured by the temporal difference between the date a specific competitive action first occurred and when the response was reported.

Response order was measured by the rank position in time of the responding firm among all responders. A firm's average response order was utilized, calculated by averaging actual rank position in the order of responders for each action. For example, if a firm responded to three actions in 1985 and its order of response to these actions was 2nd, 4th, and 6th, its average response order for 1985 would be 4th.

In terms of organizational information-processing measures, a firm's *external orientation* was inferred from the number of marketing and customer relations vice-presidents as a percentage of total vice-presidents, as listed in *World Aviation Directory*. Adams (1976) specifically identifies marketing and customer relations personnel as key external boundary personnel, and Miles and Snow (1978) relate these types of personnel to the firm's external orientation. The two measures were summed to form a single scale, labeled External Orientation ($\alpha = .68$). The assumption is that as the number of marketing and customer relations vice-presidents as a percentage of total vice-presidents increases, a firm's external orientation will also rise.

Structural complexity in the airline study was defined as the number of separate "parts" within an organization, as reflected by the division of labor and the number of levels and departments, while controlling for size. This measure is consistent with the theoretical framework developed by Bedeian (1984) and Jablin (1987). Structural complexity was operationalized as the total number of departments in the organization and the total number of officers in the company, each divided by organizational size (measured by total revenue passenger miles) for each airline, for each year. Both of these measures were obtained by counting the number of departments and officers listed in the *World Aviation Daily*. These two variables were standardized and combined by summation into a single scale, labeled Structural Complexity (α = .76). The presumption is that as the number of departments and officers in an organization increases, so too will the structural complexity.

Two components of *organizational slack* were measured in the airline study: absorbed slack, indicating the slack absorbed in the costs of organizations, and unabsorbed slack, referring to uncommitted liquid resources. As in the research of Singh (1986), absorbed slack was measured by the amount of selling, general, and administrative expenses divided by total revenue. This measure reflects slack immersed as overhead expenses, salaries, and other administrative costs. Unabsorbed slack was measured by the extent to which the sum of cash and marketable securities for the year was covered by the current liabilities (the quick ratio). This measure reflects the amount of uncommitted liquid resources. The absorbed measure of slack was obtained for each airline, for each year, from the *Air Carrier Financial Statistics*. The unabsorbed measure was obtained for each airline, for each year, directly from the *Compustat* tapes. It is assumed that airlines with a low level of slack would have fewer resources with which to engage in information-search activities.

Top management team in the airline study was defined as all corporate executives listed in the *Dun and Bradstreet Corporate*

Directory. The chief executive officer was selected, and seven other corporate executives listed in the directory were randomly chosen for each airline (there were on average 22 corporate airline executives listed in *Dun and Bradstreet* for each airline), for each year, and data were gathered on their educational levels and years of industry experience. These data were averaged for each airline, for each year, to derive a top management team score for educational level and years of experience.

Electrical Manufacturing Study

There were 22 observations from the electrical manufacturing study, one for each firm. As in the airline study, *response lag* was measured by the amount of time it took a firm to respond to a competitor's action. The amount of time was measured by the temporal difference between the date of a specific competitive action and its response.

To identify whether the organization maintained an *external orientation*, managers were asked to distribute 100 points across four functional areas in terms of the importance of each area to the organization. Relative emphasis across the four functional areas would reflect a firm's strategic orientation (Miles & Snow, 1978). The four areas are: marketing, research and development, finance and accounting, and production. As discussed above, firms focusing on marketing would be emphasizing an external market orientation and would be sensitive to external competitive actions. In addition, firms with research and development orientation generally would be more innovative, aggressive, and flexible. Such firms have also been identified as having an external orientation (Meyer, 1982; Miles & Snow, 1978). In contrast, firms that focus on finance and accounting and production can be said to have an internal orientation (Hayes & Abernathy, 1980).[5]

Structural complexity in the electrical manufacturing study was assessed by three direct and two indirect measures. Managers were asked three 5-point Likert-type questions (adapted from Smith, Mitchell, & Summer, 1985) regarding the degree to which their respective organizational structures were made complex: by rules and regulations; the fact that information had to follow formal communication procedures; and the fact that the organization followed formal budgets. Since larger organizations are generally more complex, organizational size was also included as an indirect measure. Year-end dollar sales and the number of employees were used as measures of organizational size. The internal reliability of this structural complexity measure was acceptable ($\alpha = .71$).

Data Analysis and Findings

In this section we describe only the results obtained through the formal testing of hypotheses. This presentation parallels the study-by-study description in the previous section.

Airline Study

Regression models were used to test the theory in the airline study. A separate regression model was run with imitation, likelihood, lag, and order as dependent variables.[6] Each regression equation represents the relationship between the predictor variable and the dependent variable, while holding the other independent variables constant. The results are reported in Table 5.2. The magnitude of action was included in the regression as a control variable.

As predicted, a firm's external orientation is positively related to response likelihood ($\beta = .23$; $p<.01$) and negatively related to lag ($\beta = -.32$; $p<.01$) and order ($\beta = -.17$; $p<.05$). That is, as a firm's external orientation increases, the likelihood of response increases, and response lag and order decrease. There is no support for the response imitation prediction.

In addition, as structural complexity increases, response likelihood decreases ($\beta = -.31$; $p<.001$). Moreover, structural complexity is positively related to response order; however, this relationship is only marginally significant ($\beta = .14$; $p<.10$). There is no support for other measures of response.

Table 5.2 Regression Results of Type of Action and Organizational Information-Processing Variables on Response Characteristics (standardized β coefficients reported: standard errors in parentheses; *n* = 104)

	Response Imitation	*Response Likelihood*[a]	*Response Lag*	*Response Order*
Proportion of Responses to Strategic Actions Versus Total Actions	–.039	.042	.265**	–.286**
	(.094)	(.094)	(.094)	(.093)
External Orientation	.005	.232**	–.320**	–.168*
	(.094)	(.101)	(.092)	(.093)
Structural Complexity	–.097	–.310***	–.045	.141⁺
	(.097)	(.101)	(.095)	(.096)
Absorbed Slack	–.004	–.134⁺	–.120⁺	.096
	(.096)	(.101)	(.093)	(.095)
Unabsorbed Slack	–.341**	–.085*	.043	–.056
	(.100)	(.101)	(.098)	(.099)
Years of Education	.241**	.013	.071	–.089
	(.096)	(.096)	(.094)	(.096)
Years of Experience	.031	–.203**	.041	.213**
	(.102)	(.100)	(.100)	(.101)
R^2	.19	.22	.23	.21
F-Test	3.35***	3.725***	4.11***	3.72***

⁺*p*<.10
**p*<.05
***p*<.01
****p*<.001
[a] Generalized least squares regression equation corrected for serial correlation.

There are differing levels of support for the relationship between organizational slack and response. As predicted, unabsorbed slack is negatively related to response imitation (β = -.34; *p*<.01). However, opposite the predicted relationship, unabsorbed slack is negatively related to response likelihood (β = -.10; *p*<.05). There is also a negative, but only marginally significant, relationship between absorbed slack and response lag (β = -.12; *p*<.10). This result is unexpected since firms with high absorbed slack will have few extra resources to apply to a fast response. There is no support for the relationship between slack and response order.

Finally, organizations managed by highly educated teams are more likely to imitate the actions of competitors ($\beta = .24$; $p<.01$). Years of education are unrelated to the remaining response variables. However, as expected, organizations managed by teams with fewer years of experience are more likely to respond ($\beta = -.20$; $p<.01$) and to respond early, relative to more experienced managers ($\beta = .21$; $p<.01$). Years of experience are unrelated to response imitation and response lag. Now let us consider the results from the electrical manufacturing study.

Electrical Manufacturing Study

Table 4.3 (Chapter 4) reports the regression results for the relationship between the composite measures of external orientation and structural complexity and response lag. An overall index of orientation was computed by summing the marketing and research and development orientation scores (an external orientation) and *subtracting* from that result the sum of finance and accounting and production scores (an internal orientation). A positive overall orientation score would therefore suggest an external orientation; a negative overall score would indicate an internal orientation. Just as in the airline study, the greater the external orientation, the faster the response time; the greater the internal orientation, the slower the response time ($\beta = -.35$; $p<.05$). There was no support for the relationship between structural complexity and response lag.

Table 5.3 reports the correlations relating to external orientation and response lag from the electrical manufacturing study. There is a significant negative correlation between a strategic orientation toward marketing ($r = -.511$; $p<.05$) and response time. (The correlation between research and development and response time is negative but not significant; $r = -.260$.) In contrast, there is a positive correlation, although not significant in all cases, between finance and accounting ($r = .485$; $p<.01$) and production ($r = .181$).

Table 5.4 reports the correlations between structural complexity and response time. All five measures of structural complexity

Table 5.3 Correlation of Strategic Orientation and Response Lag ($n = 22$)

Strategic Orientation	*Response Lag*
External	
marketing	−.511**
research and development	−.260
Internal	
finance and accounting	.485**
production	.181

**$p<.05$

failed to reveal any significant relationship with response time, and the signs are mixed.

Integration and Descriptive Results

Overall, the results of the formal testing of the hypotheses suggest that the underlying characteristics of firms can be important predictors of competitive response. In this section we will discuss and amplify the results with descriptive evidence from the high-technology and computer-retailing studies.

With respect to a firm's external orientation, the results suggest that firms with relatively high numbers of marketing and customer service personnel (high external orientation) will be more likely, faster, and earlier responders. Such firms will tend to have more and richer information on competitors' actions because of their ability to sense and interpret the competitive environment. One can speculate that other external activities, such as attending trade shows, will confer similar information advantages.

Many writers have criticized U.S. organizations for their lack of aggressive marketing and innovation (Hayes & Abernathy, 1980; Peters & Waterman, 1982; Reich, 1983). These writers largely attribute this problem to both an internal orientation toward efficiency and the rise of accountants and financial

Table 5.4 Correlation of Structural Complexity and Response Lag ($n = 22$)

Structural Complexity	*Response Lag*
Extent of formal structure	.085
Extent of structured communications	.161
Extent of structured budgets	−.074
Organizational size in dollar sales	.236
Organizational size in number of employees	−.059

managers into top-level management roles. The present research found that firms with internal orientations toward finance/accounting and production respond slowly to competitor actions, which is suggestive of a lack of aggressiveness.

The results related to structural complexity are also important. In particular, they suggest that specialization (part of the measure of complexity) may not be helpful in responding to environmental changes (e.g., actions by competitors). Perhaps firms need to find mechanisms to harness the advantages of this complexity (e.g., achieve integration) or they may need to strive for more structural simplicity. It is interesting that structural complexity was unrelated to response lag in both studies. It may be that today's information systems allow firms to be responsive despite the complexity of their structures.

The findings are mixed concerning organizational slack. The negative relationship between unabsorbed slack and response likelihood may suggest that firms with unabsorbed slack feel that they have a *buffer* to environmental changes and have less pressure/need to respond. The negative relationship between absorbed slack and response lag may be a little more complex than assumed. For example, absorbed slack would include the costs related to marketing and customer relations vice-presidents (the external orientation measure). As a result, some of the absorbed slack may be invested in mechanisms that help the firm respond more quickly, such as obtaining more and richer information.

The management team result portrays a novice management team attempting to be more forceful in the marketplace. It is possible that inexperienced managers are either more sensitive to environmental changes or more capable of creating organizational change.

The formal tests of the hypotheses discussed above do not consider the mechanisms by which firms learn of rivals' actions. However, as suggested in the overall communication theory presented in Chapter 1, the channel through which a firm first discovers a competitor's move is also likely to influence response. This working hypothesis was examined with data from the high-technology study. As discussed previously, early discovery of a competitor's move can greatly facilitate a response. For example, a firm that is forewarned of a competitor's move may have sufficient time to respond appropriately, whereas a firm may respond inappropriately when it is surprised and quickly moves to respond. There are a number of channels or mechanisms through which a firm can learn of its competitors' moves; these include hearing competitors' announcements, talking to customers, talking to one's own sales force, reading advertisements, or experiencing a decline in sales. All of these learning mechanisms can be expected to have differential impacts on response, particularly response lag.

As shown in Table 5.5, among high-technology firms there is a strong relationship between the channel through which a firm learns about a competitor's move and the speed of a firm's response. Managers who recognized a competitor's move by experiencing a decline in sales, by seeing the competitor's advertising, or by talking with customers took considerably longer to respond than did managers who learned of the move by reading competitor announcements or heard about it through their own sales force. However, managers most often learned of competitor moves through these three slower, less direct techniques. For example, 83% of the managers learned of competitor moves by talking to customers, reading advertising, or experiencing a decline in sales, and the associated average response time was more than 8 months. Only 17% of the managers

Table 5.5 The Relationship Between the Mechanism Through Which the Firm Learned of the Action and Response Lag

Learning Mechanism	*Number of Firms*	*Percentage*	*Response Lag (in months)*
Competitor announcements	2	8.5	1
Own sales force	2	8.5	5
Customers	10	44.0	8
Advertising or marketing	5	22.0	7.6
Experienced a drop in sales	4	17.0	8.8
	23	100.0	

learned of moves by reading competitor announcements or through their own sales force, but these managers responded relatively quickly, averaging only 3 months. As Porter (1980) suggests, firms should keep a close watch on competitor announcements and should encourage their sales people to provide feedback to management on the activities of competitors.

As with competitive actions reported in Chapter 4, the relationship between channels of communication (how the action was learned) and response was found to be more complex in the computer-retailing study. More specifically, firms seem to learn of competitors' actions through multiple sources. For example, firms responding to pricing actions typically obtain their information from published advertisements (65%) and customers (29%). Moreover, the information on new promotional campaigns of rivals was most often learned from suppliers (50%), advertisements (33%), and directly from customers (17%).

Another important area concerns the goals of rivals. From an information-processing perspective, goals assist managers in deciding what information to either scrutinize or ignore (Locke & Latham, 1990). All things being equal, managers will be more likely to sense, select, and retain information that is directly related to their goals (Locke & Latham). Therefore, moves threatening the accomplishment of specific goals will elicit greater

Table 5.6 The Relationship Between the Goal of the Responding Firm and Response Lag

Goal of the Responding Firm	*Number of Firms*	*Percentage*	*Response Lag (in months)*
Profit improvement goal	7	28	13.62
Sales growth goal	13	52	6.14
Means or strategy goals	5	20	6.67
	25	100	

information-processing activity and quicker responses than moves that do not threaten the attainment of specific goals. Porter (1980) suggests that a firm should avoid strategic acts that will touch off warfare or direct confrontation by threatening a competitor's ability to achieve key goals.

Table 5.6 highlights the relationship between the responding firm's goals and its response time, as studied in the high-technology study. As suggested by information theory and by Porter (1980), the goals of the firm do appear to influence the speed with which it responds. Managers of each firm identified their goals, which the authors classified into three groups: profit goals (such as improving ROI or ROA); sales growth goals (such as improving sales or market share); and means or strategy goals (such as improving quality or employee morale). Firms with sales goals responded more than twice as fast to competitor moves as did firms with profit goals (6.14 months versus 13.62 months). Firms with profit goals appear to be leery of responding quickly, for fear of provoking warfare that would threaten profits. Firms with strategic goals also responded swiftly, perhaps because they were not overly concerned that a potential escalation would interfere with this objective.

Research Questions

This chapter focused on an aspect of competitor analysis: the identification of a set of organizational variables that would predict response. More specifically, the chapter examined the relationship between information-processing characteristics of responding firms and their response behavior. In each of the studies reported, there was support for the general hypothesis that information-processing characteristics of the responding firm influence the manner by which it responds. For example, fast responders have a greater external orientation toward the market, tend to have sales goals, and pay closer attention to competitor announcements than do slow responders. Similarly, early responders have greater external orientations, less structural complexity, and less experienced top management teams than do late responders. In addition, likely responders have a greater external orientation, less structural complexity, less experienced management teams, and lower levels of slack resources than do firms that are less prone to respond. Finally, imitative responders will be managed by highly educated top management teams and have low levels of unabsorbed slack.

While the results begin to contribute to a predictive model of response, additional research is necessary. Table 5.7 summarizes the future research questions raised by the findings presented in this chapter.

Most important, additional research is needed to determine if there is a more robust and parsimonious set of predictors of response. The present research has identified a number of predictors, but many were found to have differential impacts. For example, external orientation predicted response order, lag, and likelihood but not imitation; years of management experience predicted likelihood and response order but not response lag or imitation. Thus, one area of future research should be the identification of a set of organizational variables that would more accurately and efficiently predict response. Examples of additional indicators include: attendance at trade shows; membership in industry associations; functional backgrounds of members of top management teams; the actual level of sophistication in information-processing of each firm; and the actual level of competitor analysis or environmental monitoring carried out in each firm. Many of these measures can be thought

Table 5.7 Future Research Questions

1. What is the most accurate and efficient set of organizational predictors of response?
2. Is there a set of predictors that will be equally effective in predicting different dimensions of response (e.g., response likelihood, response timing, and so on)?
3. What is the influence of attending trade shows; membership in industry associations, functional backgrounds of members of top management teams; the actual level of sophistication in information-processing; and the level of competitor analysis or environmental monitoring carried out in each firm on response?
4. What organizational predictors of response have curvilinear and multiplicative effects on response?
5. Will a firm with an internal orientation or high levels of structural complexity be more likely to respond with pricing actions than will a firm with an external orientation?
6. Will a firm with an external orientation and less structural complexity be more inclined to respond with innovative actions?
7. Will a firm with high levels of slack resources be more capable of responding with strategic actions than will firms without such resources?
8. Will experienced top management teams be more capable of responding with strategic actions, which require more expertise to implement, than less experienced management teams?

of as additional indicators of absorbed slack or the investment of slack resources into the firm to enhance response.

However, as the search for predictors of response continues, researchers must be careful to select indicators that are readily available for managers to use in their own competitor analyses. For example, the indicators used in the current research can for the most part be obtained from publicly available information sources. The identification of predictors of response that are not available for managerial use would have little practical value.

Future research can also build upon the present research effort by considering more complex combinations of response predictors. Certain relationships may well be curvilinear and multiplicative. For example, it is possible that while a greater degree of external orientation will enhance response up to a point, too much of an external orientation may impede response by creating excessive competitive information and information overload. In addition, while very experienced management may be reluctant and slow to respond, a management team with too little experience may make the implementation of some kinds of response impractical. Thus, there may be a point at which the benefits of a particular organizational capability become a liability in responding.

Concerning multiplicative effects, it would be logical to expect that structural complexity will not impede response if the firm has abundant slack resources to overcome complexity, for example, if the firm invests heavily in sophisticated information-processing. Moreover, externally oriented firms with less structural complexity and low levels of management experience could be expected to be more aggressive in responding than firms with just one or two of these characteristics. Further research directed at identifying the most important predictors of response and the degree to which interactions are present would be helpful.

Another area of future research is predicting the actual manner or type of response. One can hypothesize that a firm with an internal orientation or high levels of structural complexity will be more inclined to respond with pricing actions than will a firm with an external orientation; pricing actions are relatively simple to implement. Conversely, a firm with an external orientation and less structural complexity should be more capable and thus more inclined to respond with innovative actions. Similarly, firms with high levels of slack resources should be more capable of responding with strategic actions, which require more resources, than will firms without sufficient slack. Moreover, experienced top management teams may be more capable of responding with strategic actions, which require more expertise to implement, than will less experienced management teams.

In conclusion, researchers can obtain a more complete picture of competitive interaction and advantage by focusing their attention on the variables that predict response. Such an orientation can directly contribute to a model of competitor analysis that will be of benefit to practicing managers. While the research reported in this chapter has provided an important contribution, further research is needed to improve our understanding of what factors best predict a rival's response.

Notes

1. Note that this perspective is quite consistent with the concept of barriers to entry or barriers to mobility (Porter, 1980).

2. All of these response measures are tested with airline data. In addition, response lag is tested with data from the Electrical Manufacturing Study.

3. Although it could be argued that more exhaustive search procedures employed by less experienced managers would delay response, the aggressiveness factor is expected to outweigh the time delay potentially experienced by utilizing more extensive search.

4. This unit of analysis is appropriate for several reasons. First, using average response scores takes into account the interdependence inherent in a single firm's responses during a given year (Glick & Roberts, 1984). Statistically, the variance between organizations and across time on each of the response measures is significantly greater than the variation within organizations and within a given year. Further, this approach is conceptually consistent with Porter's (1980) notion of response profiles. Thus, the response measures provide a portrait of the organization's typical response behavior during a given year. Finally, aggregation of response behavior in a given year is necessary for consistency with organizational and performance data, which are available only on an annual basis. The alternative to this procedure would be to use each competitive event as a unit of analysis. However, annual organizational and performance data would then have to be duplicated to match each event of a given year. While this would significantly add to the number of cases, Glick & Roberts point out that "all reported significant tests would be overly liberal" (pg. 725). Thus the hypotheses will be tested with yearly average response scores, arguably a conservative approach.

5. To corroborate this measure, managers were asked to distribute an additional 100 points across the same four variables (marketing, research and development, accounting and finance, and production). This time, however, the 100 points were to be representative of the top-level management team's experience and training. It was theorized that the most important function in a firm would be reflective of the top-level team members' experience and training. For example, if all members of the top-level management team were trained in marketing, they were asked to distribute 100 points to marketing. The firm's most important function was highly correlated with top-level team members' experience and training (marketing: $r = .49$, $p<.01$; research and development: $r = .78$, $p<.001$; accounting and finance: $r = .39$, $p<.01$; and production: $r = .61$, $p<.001$). That is, firms that identified their most important function as marketing

and/or research and development (an external orientation) had top-level teams composed of managers with backgrounds in marketing and research and development. In contrast, firms that identified their most important function as accounting and finance, and/or production (an internal orientation) were managed by executives with backgrounds in finance, accounting, and production.

6. Because of the potential problem of serial correlation with time series data, a Durbin-Watson test statistic was calculated for each regression equation. For the regression equations predicting imitation, lag, and order, there was no indication of serial correlation; the Durbin-Watson tests were 2.00, 1.89, and 2.02, respectively. In the regression with response likelihood as the dependent variable, the Durbin-Watson test yielded a value of 1.53—indeterminate with regard to the existence of serial correlation. Consistent with procedures employed by Harrigan (1982), a generalized least squares technique was used. First, an estimate of the serial correlation present in the sample was obtained from the initial ordinary least squares regression. Generalized differencing corrections to all the variables were then applied, and a generalized least squares equation was estimated. Pindyck and Rubinfeld (1981) provide full details of the procedure. The Durbin-Watson Test statistic from the generalized least squares equation indicated no serial correlation (Durbin-Watson Test = 2.01). The response likelihood generalized regression results did not differ substantially from the least squares results.

6

Industry Environments and Rivalry

THE various competitive actions and reactions of firms to one another represent an important part of an industry's environment. For example, in some industries the pattern of moves and countermoves can be highly unstable and unpredictable, a situation that leaves the entire industry worse off in terms of profits. In other industries the framework of rivalry can be more predictable, genteel, and profitable. Porter (1980) and other economists have forcefully argued that the manner in which firms jockey for position is a critical industry force impacting both firm and overall industry profitability.

AUTHORS' NOTE: This chapter was co-authored with Greg Young and August Shomberg. Portions were adapted from "Building Competitive Advantage in Diverse Industries," Proceedings of the Second International Conference on Managing the High Technology Firm: Strategic Leadership in High Technology Organizations, Michael Lawless and Luis Gomez-Mejia (eds.), University of Colorado at Boulder, January 10-12, 1990, pp. 137-141.

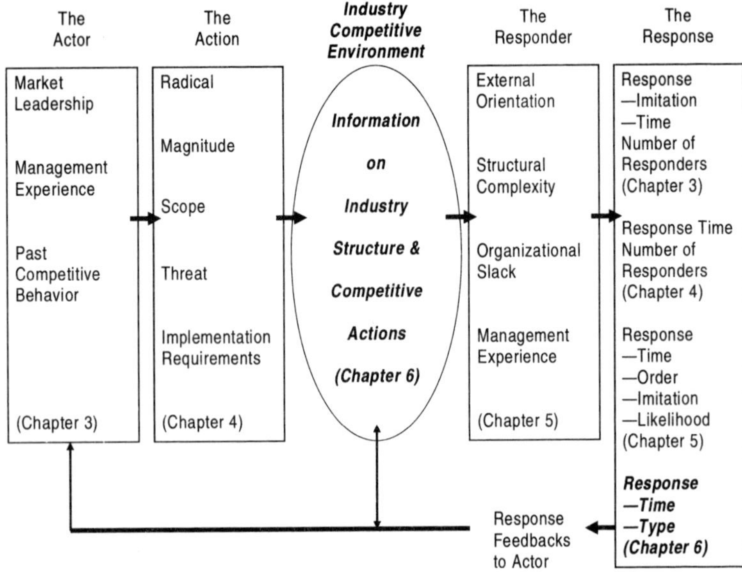

Figure 6.1. The Focus of Chapter 6

This chapter examines rivalry in three diverse industries. More specifically, the extent of rivalry in the fragmented computer-retailing industry, the emerging growth high-technology industry, and the mature domestic airline industry is compared and contrasted. A central argument of the chapter is that differences in rivalry across industries are a function of the amount and quality of competitive information available in the industry.

Figure 6.1 links the emphasis of this chapter on industry environments to the encompassing communication model presented in Chapter 1. First, we identify six key dimensions along which industry environments can differ. These dimensions are then used to predict variation in rivalry across the industries. Inferences about rivalry are made in terms of the magnitude of actions and reactions, the degree of imitative responses, and the speed of responses across the three industries. Since the chapter compares the degree of rivalry across the different studies, it also serves to integrate results highlighted in previous chapters.

Characteristics of Industry Environments

The environment can be a crucial determinant of a firm's survival (Aldrich, 1979; Hannan & Freeman, 1977; Thompson, 1967). Indeed, it is well recognized that as rivalry increases, industry profitability decreases (Bettis & Weeks, 1987; Kwoka & Ravenscraft, 1986; Porter, 1980; Scherer & Ross, 1990). However, environments can differ substantially across industries (Dess & Beard, 1984; Lawrence & Lorsch, 1967). Six key dimensions by which industries can vary include:

dynamism, which concerns the *rate of industry change* (Aldrich, 1979; Cool & Schendel, 1987; Dess & Beard, 1984; Emery & Trist, 1965);

uncertainty, which pertains to the *predictability* of industry events (Emery & Trist, 1965; Hinnings, Hickson, Pennings, & Schneck, 1974; Thompson, 1967);

complexity, which relates to the number of different organizationally *relevant* attributes in the industry (Child, 1974; Dess & Beard, 1984; Pennings, 1975);

resource scarcity, which refers to the extent to which the industry is *lean in terms of needed resources* (Aldrich, 1979; Cool & Schendel, 1987; Emery & Trist, 1965; Mann, 1966; Thompson, 1967);

homogeneity, which alludes to the *similarity of competitors* in terms of size, resources, strategies, and costs (Aldrich, 1979; Gollop & Roberts, 1979; Hannan & Freeman, 1977); and

interconnectedness, which deals with the extent to which events or components of the industry are *organized and interrelated* (Aldrich, 1979; Emery & Trist, 1965; Gollop & Roberts, 1979; Jurkovich, 1974).

These six dimensions are used to describe three generic industry environments: emerging growth, mature, and fragmented.

Emerging growth industries are generally newly formed industries that are based on technical innovations. The key characteristics of the emerging growth industry is that there are "no rules to the competitive game." Such industries are dynamic and uncertain, that is, they are characterized by high and unpredictable rates of change. This extreme uncertainty and unpredictability are often caused by the high rates of innovation of firms in the industry, lack of established industry standards, and the large numbers of competitors seeking the potential profits and resources of a new industry (Gort & Klepper, 1982). Moreover, the perceived high potential of the industry will attract many new entrants, who, at least in the early stage of the industry, will benefit from low entry barriers. All of these factors will mean that firms will be heterogeneous in terms of size, capabilities, resources, and strategies. Scherer and Ross (1990) note that when competitors are diverse, they will have difficulty coordinating their actions; there will be low interconnectedness and high complexity.

In contrast, *mature industries* are far less dynamic and more predictable. That is, the rate of change is slower and more certain. By definition, such an industry experiences low or negative rates of growth and, consequently, is not as attractive to new entrants. Competitors in mature industries are generally fewer, more homogeneous, and better known to one another. The rules of competition will have been established by rivals with years of experience with one another, which will create significant interconnectedness. In addition, industry barriers and standards will have been well established. All of the above suggest the industry will be far less complex and more predictable.

A *fragmented industry* is one in which no firm has the dominant market share, or one where no firm can strongly influence industry outcomes. Typical industries in this category include retailing, services, and distribution. Such industries generally have an absence of economies of scale, low overall entry barriers, high transportation and inventory costs, low overhead, and local management ownership and control.

In terms of environments, fragmented industries represent some key features of both mature and emerging growth industries. Fragmented industries typically are less dynamic and unpredictable than emerging growth industries, but more so than mature industries. As a result of low barriers to entry, there are often many small competitors of approximately equal size. Likewise, competitors are more diverse and heteroge-

Table 6.1 Environmental Characteristics of Three Industries

	Emerging Growth Industry	*Fragmented Industry*	*Mature Industry*
Dynamism	high	moderate	low
Uncertainty	high	moderate	low
Complexity	high	moderate	low
Munificence	high	moderate	low
Homogeneity	low	high	high
Interconnectedness	low	low	high

neous than in mature industries. In this regard fragmented industries resemble complex emerging growth industries; however, fragmented industries, in contrast to emerging growth and mature industries, often face geographically unique markets where the rules of competition and degree of interconnectedness are often determined within each market segment. This makes local control and local management very important. Table 6.1 summarizes the key structural dimensions of each generic industry.

Characteristics of Environments and Rivalry

As noted, this chapter focuses on three dimensions of rivalry: magnitude of action, degree of imitation in response, and speed of response. In this section of the chapter we argue that variation across industries in terms of the six environmental characteristics will influence rivalry primarily through the manner in which competitive information is available to decision makers. Information can, among other dimensions, vary in amount, variety, and reliability (Daft & Lengel, 1984).

Generally speaking, and relative to other industries, actions in emerging growth industries will be of greater magnitude as firms attempt to differentiate and set the standard. Also, responses will be more imitative because firms will be fearful of being left behind, and response times will be swift. The logic for the latter hypothesis begins with the observation that the extreme dynamism and uncertainty in emerging growth industries will create a setting in which information on rivals' intentions, capabilities, and actions will be uncertain, incomplete, and unreliable. Under these conditions, firms will often be forced to act and respond blindly, motivated by a fear of losing ground. As noted, high growth rates will make the industry attractive to new entrants, and the diverse nature of current competitors will lead to an increased variety of information as to the most profitable course of action. Many firms may suffer from information overload if there is too much competitive information to make effective decisions. The lack of reliable information on market interconnectedness or an inability of firms to have perfect information on the causes and consequences of actions will add to the uncertainty. Moreover, the variety of information embedded in technological developments in emerging industries indicates a lack of standards, which compels firms to compete in order to have their technology become the industry norm. Drawing from Schumpeter (1950), Porac and Thomas (1990) describe how firms in this situation face the dual pressures of differentiation, that is, taking risks to be different from competitors—and imitation, that is, avoiding risks by following competitors.

In contrast to emerging growth industries, actions in mature industries will be of lower magnitude, and responses will be more imitative but slow. The lower levels of dynamism and uncertainty in mature industries will make competitive information more certain, reliable, and available. Standards will have been set in years past, and competitors will have substantial experience with one another. The low profit potential of the industry will make it less attractive to new entrants. Firms will become risk adverse, thus avoiding actions that require major commitments of resources. Since there will be fewer competitors of more equal size (homogeneous), firm strategies and capabilities will be more equal, and thus pricing will become the key variable. It is likely that firms will have sufficient information to recognize cause and effect relationships and to coordinate their actions with rivals (Scherer & Ross, 1990).

Rivalry in fragmented industries in terms of such dimensions will be midway between the extremes of emerging and mature industries. Although they are more dynamic and uncertain than mature industries, fragmented industries combine established standards, competitors of more equal size, and clear rules of competition, thus making information more available and reliable than in emerging growth industries. Consequently, the extent of rivalry will be greater than in mature industries but less than in high-technology emerging growth industries.

Measures

The results of four independent studies conducted in three industry environments are compared and contrasted to explore the general predictions presented above. Details of the different methods employed in each study can be found in Chapter 2; measures were defined as follows.

Generic Industry Environments. Porter (1980) identifies a number of generic industry environments, including fragmented, emerging growth, and mature. Three different industries, reflective of each of these different generic industry environments, were selected for the current research.

As discussed above, a fragmented industry is one in which no firm has the dominant market share, or where no firm can strongly influence industry outcomes. Typical industries in this category include retailing, services, and distribution. Such industries generally have an absence of economies of scale, low overall entry barriers, high transportation and inventory costs, low overhead, and local management ownership and control. The personal computer retailing industry fits this description closely and is used to represent a fragmented industry in this research project. The total market share of the top four firms in this industry is less than 20%.

As noted, emerging growth industries are generally newly formed industries that have evolved out of technical innovations, and their key characteristic is that there are "no rules to the competitive game." In the middle 1980s the electrical manufacturing industry and the electronic high-technology industry fit this description closely and are used in the present research. For firms in these two industries the average rate of growth in revenue and profits exceeded 22% in the year prior to the study.

Industries mature over time, especially as competitors develop years of experience with one another. The U.S. domestic airline industry has matured substantially over the years. In particular, the industry has been largely dominated by the same participants for almost five decades, and there have been no dramatic technological changes since deregulation in 1978; therefore, it is used to represent the mature industry in this research.

Magnitude of Action. As discussed more fully in Chapter 4, magnitude of action was defined as strategic or tactical. Strategic actions involve major commitments of resources that are difficult to reverse once implemented; tactical actions involve fewer commitments of resources and they can be reversed more easily. Six experts were asked to distinguish strategic actions from tactical actions, using the definitions provided above. There was virtually unanimous agreement among the judges in the classification of the actions into the two categories.

Response Imitation. As elaborated in Chapter 2, response imitation concerns the degree of concurrence between the action type and the response type. An imitation score was created to measure the degree of duplication involved in each response. This score was calculated so that when the type of response was the same as the type of action (for example, a price cut in response to a price cut), the imitation score equaled 1; when the response type was not the same as the action type (for example, a price cut in response to a new product introduction), the imitation score equaled 0.

Response Lag. As outlined in Chapter 2, response lag was measured by the amount of time it took a firm to respond to a competitor's action. The amount of time was measured by the temporal difference between the date a specific competitive action was first reported and the date of the response.

Results

Formal statistical tests of differences across the four studies are not applicable, given the different methods employed, the small number of cases when the industry is used as the unit of analysis, and the exploratory nature of this aspect of the research. Nonetheless, simple comparisons of mean scores are useful in explaining differences in competitive interaction across disparate industry environments.

The specific actions firms take with regard to one another vary substantially across industries. For example, promotion actions are dominant in computer retailing, while pricing actions rule the airline industry. In contrast, new product introductions are the norm in electrical manufacturing and high-technology industries. Moreover, as can be observed in Table 6.2, there is substantial variation in the magnitude of actions across the four industries. Actions appear more likely to be of major magnitude in emerging growth industries. In the electrical manufacturing and the high-technology studies, 81% and 44%, respectively, of the actions were strategic, compared to 15% in computer retailing and 16% in airlines. The major strategic actions in the airline industry involve opening new hubs; in computer retailing they involve new entry by competitors; and in the high-technology industry they concern new product introductions. Perhaps the strong orientation toward actions of major magnitude in high-technology industries reflects the race to develop technical standards associated with high research and development expenses. In the emerging stages of this industry's development, firms are jockeying in an intense and perhaps risky way to define product markets, build barriers,

Table 6.2 Comparison of Magnitude of Action, Degree of Imitation, Response Times, and Performance

	Type of Industry			
	Emerging Growth Industry		*Fragmented Industry*	*Mature Industry*
	Electrical Mfg.	*High-Tech*	*Computer-Retailing*	*Domestic Airlines*
Type of Action				
Percentage of Strategic Actions	81%	44%	15%	16%
Percentage of Tactical Actions	19%	56%	85%	84%
Percentage of Imitative Responses	64%	36%	70%	82%
Response Times				
Strategic	271 days	540 days	47 days	34 days
Tactical	124 days	165 days	24 days	8 days

and establish standards. In contrast, rivalry in computer retailing and the airline industry is primarily of lesser magnitude; 85% of the actions in computer retailing and 84% of those of the airlines are tactical. This outcome is logical, given that most of the standards and barriers would have been created in years past.

Contrary to expectations, firms appear less likely to imitate the actions of rivals in emerging growth environments. In the electrical manufacturing study the percentage of response imitation was only 36%, while in the electronic high-technology study it was 64%. Both of these percentages are lower than in computer retailing (70%) and airlines (79%). These results can be partially explained by the difficulty in imitating strategic actions of greater magnitude, which require unique resources or assets. Moreover, the extreme uncertainty in high-technology industries makes the outcomes of most major actions uncertain; that is, they may be viewed as too risky to imitate, at least initially, and this is particularly true of strategic actions of major magnitude. In the race to set standards, imitation may signal a rival's acceptance of a standard, something most rivals would want to avoid.

There are also substantial differences in the time it takes for competitors to respond across the three industries. Overall, responses to actions of major magnitude take longer than responses to actions of lower magnitude. This is to be expected because major actions are likely to evoke significant responses, which require more time to implement. In addition, since strategic actions require more resources, they may be viewed as carrying greater risk. Thus rivals may take a "wait and see" attitude before responding. A salient finding is that response times are measured in months and years in emerging growth industries, whereas in computer retailing and airlines, response is measured in hours and days. For example, response time to strategic actions in the electrical manufacturing and high-technology industries averages 271 days and 540 days, respectively. In contrast, response times to strategic actions in computer retailing and the domestic airlines are 47 days and 34 days, respectively. These differences may again be explained by the race to set industry standards, because a competitor would feel compelled to respond only after an action results in a standard. Such standards would naturally take time to establish.

However, this rationale cannot be applied to explain the differences in response times to tactical moves. Response times across industries are similar to those for strategic moves. In computer retailing and in the airline industry, response times to tactical actions are swift, averaging 24 and 8 days, respectively. In contrast, tactical response times in emerging growth industries are remarkably slow, averaging 124 days and 165 days. Perhaps high industry unpredictability and resulting information uncertainty are forcing competitors to postpone a response until this uncertainty is reduced. For example, a competitor may not have the information to judge the effectiveness of a rival's tactical price cut when it is first introduced. Thus, the responding firm may wish to wait in order to gather additional information before committing to a response. In contrast, competitors in the airline and computer-retailing industry probably can better anticipate the results of a rival's price cut, thus allowing the firm to respond swiftly.

In summary, rivalry is somewhat similar in the fragmented computer-retailing industry and the mature domestic airlines industry, but very different from that observed among emerging growth firms. Major differences include the following:

- Firms in emerging growth industries tend to initiate proportionately more actions and responses of greater magnitude than do firms in fragmented or mature industries;
- Response imitation is proportionately lower in emerging growth industries than in fragmented and mature industries; and
- Response times in emerging growth industries are substantially slower than in fragmented and mature industries.

One way of explaining the results reported above is by considering the levels of competitive information processing across the different industries.

Processing Competitor Information in Diverse Industries

For emerging growth firms, the study portrays a relatively docile competitive environment. That is, compared with the more mature airline industry and the fragmented computer-retailing industry, emerging growth firms face less tactical rivalry, fewer imitative responses, and longer response times by rivals. These factors must be considered generally favorable. Interestingly, most managers from emerging growth firms also suffer from competitive information inadequacy; many do not believe that competitors exist until they are adversely affected by a rival's action. In addition, there is no common or organized information source from which managers can learn of a rival's action. Moreover, business customers tend to predominate, so that information on price and other conditions of sale are much less available than for retail sales in industries such as airlines and personal computers.

Also important, the competitive information conditions are just the opposite in the airline industry and the computer retailing industry. In the airline industry, *Aviation Daily* reports the actions of all airlines to one another on a daily basis, and the on-line computer reservation systems provide almost instantaneous information on the pricing actions of competitors. American Airlines' and United Airlines' 2-day response to TWA's price cuts in more than 300 markets was made possible by the fact that these rivals can identify competitive price changes almost immediately in their own industry-wide computer reservation systems. That is, all airlines operate computer reservation systems and list any rate changes directly in these systems; such changes are instantly available across all computer reservation systems.

Similarly, managers from computer-retailing firms analyze the actions of competitors by tracking newspaper advertisements and subscribing to regularly scheduled market research products where the pricing and promotional activities of all competitors are listed. For example, in the Washington, D.C., market, the *Washington Post*'s weekly business supplement lists the price and promotional information of virtually all the local computer retailers for the current week. As in the airline industry, managers are extremely knowledgeable about what their competitors are doing. This information abundance, in fact, may be a more important explanation of differences in rivalry than the structure of the generic industry environment in which firms operate.

This discussion supports one of the major themes of this book: A firm must maintain information on a competitor's plans and actions and be prepared to respond appropriately. However, a firm's ability and desire to keep track of competitors is likely to be a function of the environment in which it operates. In particular, in some environments it will be extremely difficult to track competitors' intentions and behaviors. Firms in such industries must retain the flexibility to act and react as the competitive environment changes.

Research Questions

The research in this chapter has compared the level of rivalry in three different industries. Although the results are important, they are preliminary in nature. Future research can proceed in many directions, including investigating the specific structural determinants of rivalry *within* an industry, the degree of rivalry in other diverse industries, and the relationship between rivalry and the level of competitor information available to firms in an industry.

Future research is needed on the level of rivalry in other industries. For example, one can examine the magnitude of action, the degree of imitation, and the speed of response in other generic industry environments, such as industries in decline. Moreover, the results of this study need to be replicated in other industries that could also be classified as emerging growth, fragmented, and mature. Examining rivalry in a more complete set of industries, with various underlying structural conditions, will enhance our understanding of industry evolution and dynamic strategy.

Research should also directly measure characteristics of different industry structure, such as number of competitors, amount of fixed costs, cost differential, and so on. The idea would be to link measures of industry structure to the specific measures of rivalry. One would expect, for example, that as the number of competitors in an industry increases, so too will the speed of responses and the degree of imitation.

Finally, this research has utilized information-processing theory to explain the differences in rivalry across the three industries. However, the actual level of the processing of competitive information in firms has not been directly assessed. Thus, information-processing and availability could be linked with the actual level of rivalry in these industries. For example, the extent of industry sophistication in competitor analysis, the coverage of competitor actions and reactions in industry publications, and the existence of industry associations could be linked with magnitude of actions, the degree of imitation, and the speed of response. One hypothesis would be that when the information-processing capabilities of industries are very high, rivalry will be very high or low. Rivalry will be high until competitors learn to use this information capability to tacitly coordinate their activities. When information-processing capabilities of rivals in an industry are low, competition will be moderate.

In conclusion, the comparison of four studies suggests that the effects of industry context on rivalry is important. However, the results indicate that additional theory and empirical research are needed.

Postscript

In a recent and ongoing study of three different types of industries, the preliminary evidence indicates that the results are similar to those described in this chapter. In the brewing industry the average response time to new product introductions was 4.9 years, and the average number of responders was 2.8; in the telecommunications industry the corresponding figures were 3.25 years and 1.9 responders; and in the computer industry they were 2.30 years and 5.10 responders.

7

Competitive Moves, Responses, and Organizational Performance

FIRMS undertake actions in order to enhance or protect profits in relation to their rivals. For example, a firm can seek to improve profits by introducing an innovative advertising campaign. Profits may be enhanced to the extent that customers respond favorably to the advertising, and rivals are delayed in responding. However, as described in previous chapters, the first mover can attract customers from rivals only until such time as the visible profits of the first mover and the losses experienced by the non-responder motivate the latter to respond and imitate. When rivals quickly imitate a firm's actions, the potential profits may have to be shared; there may be no gain for either player; or profits may be adversely affected for each contestant.

This chapter examines empirically the performance consequences of move time and order in competitive rivalry. It focuses primarily on the timing and order of easy-to-imitate moves. Most of the first mover literature has emphasized difficult-to-imitate moves. The emphasis in this chapter is chiefly on easy-to-imitate competitive moves, such as price cuts, advertising campaigns, and service promotions. Porter (1990) has labeled such relatively simple actions as *lower order moves*.

In the first section of this chapter we present a model predicting that fast and early movers will outperform slow and late movers. Potential confounds are discussed and a set of control variables is identified. Finally, the theory is tested with a data set composed of 191 easy-to-imitate competitive moves in the U.S. domestic airline industry. In the integration and discussion sections of the chapter we support the results obtained from the airline industry, with performance findings obtained in our studies of difficult-to-imitate moves among high technology and electrical manufacturing firms.

Moving Early Versus Late in Rivalry

A number of writers have focused their attention on the advantages of being a *first mover* (Eaton & Ware, 1987; Gal-Or, 1985; Glazer, 1985; Lieberman & Montgomery, 1988), a *pioneer* (Boulding & Moore, 1987; Robinson, 1988; Robinson & Fornell, 1985; Schnaars, 1986), or an *early entrant* (Eaton & Ware, 1987; Farrell & Saloner, 1986; Fudenberg, Gilbert, Stiglitz, & Tirole, 1983). As discussed in Chapter 1, the first mover achieves advantage because of the temporary monopolistic position obtained by acting ahead of rivals (Nelson & Winter, 1982). From this temporary asymmetrical position, the first moving firm can build advantages by exploiting learning curve effects, research and development improvements, preemption of scarce resources, and the creation of buyer switching costs (Lieberman & Montgomery). However, a central characteristic determining the size of the first mover advantage is the relative ease with which rivals can imitate the action (Lieberman & Montgomery, 1988).

While there is a growing body of literature on first mover advantages, the focus has been on difficult-to-imitate, high-order moves, such as the creation of an industry (Xerox) or the introduction of a significant product innovation (Polaroid). There has been no empirical research on the issue of whether firms should move first in everyday or ordinary competition, where rivals can often imitate more quickly. Yet, according to Porter (1990), it is precisely in this context that firms must struggle most often to build and sustain competitive advantage.

Firms build advantage by taking offensive and defensive moves against their rivals (Porter, 1980). However, "Competitive moves by one firm have noticeable effects on its competitors and thus may incite retaliation or efforts to counter the move; that is, firms are mutually dependent" (Porter, p. 17). As noted above, the first mover can draw customers from opponents only until such time as the profits earned by the first mover and the penalties experienced by the non-responder agitate the latter to respond and imitate.

Indeed, it is the possibility of imitation which gives rise to the disadvantages of moving first. Lieberman and Montgomery detail these disadvantages. In particular, they note that to imitate a rival's actions involves less risk and uncertainty than to move first. Moving first involves significant risk since seldom does the first moving firm know, a priori, how successful its actions will be (Scherer & Ross, 1990; Wernerfelt & Karnani, 1987). For example, customers may ignore a price cut if they perceive the action as a sign of inferior quality. Moreover, uncertain and rapidly changing customer needs may create disadvantages for the first mover since later movers may be better positioned to provide a more appropriate product or service fit (Lieberman & Montgomery). For example, the first moving firm may get locked into an extended TV advertising campaign that later rivals can use as a starting point for more effective campaigns. Further, "incumbent inertia" may block the first moving firms from making slight modifications to enhance product/service fit (Cooper & Schendel, 1976; Lieberman & Montgomery, 1988).

The "fast second" strategy has been emphasized as a medium to achieve the fundamental advantages of moving first while mitigating the potential disadvantages (Baldwin & Childs, 1969; Gal-Or, 1985; Kamien & Schwartz, 1978; Katz & Shapiro, 1987; Scherer & Ross, 1990; Teece, 1986). Drawing from Scherer (1967), Baldwin and Childs explicitly modeled the case in which fast imitation is more profitable than acting first and labeled this proposal the "fast second" strategy. More recently, Teece (1986), Katz and Shapiro (1987), and Scherer and Ross have studied the conditions under which the fast second strategy is a desirable alternative to innovation.

The firm using a fast second strategy benefits primarily from cost savings derived from superior information. Baldwin and Childs noted that it may be cheaper and quicker for a rival to examine a first mover's experience with a new action than it would be to experiment and test a new action independently. For example, by simply copying a rival's new service innovation, a firm may avoid the development and testing costs. Moreover, by observing that a first mover's price cut was perceived as a sign of poor quality, rivals can avoid matching the price cut, thus enhancing their own profits. In addition, the fast second firm may possess enough information so that it can learn in a relatively inexpensive manner from a rival's mistakes and improve upon the action. The first to act will undoubtedly experience problems or glitches as the implementation of the move proceeds. Such snafus will provide opportunities for the fast second firm to do better.

Figure 7.1, drawn in a modified version from Scherer and Ross, portrays two alternative move scenarios. First, consider the move implemented at T* in Case 1. Assume that the move is unprofitable because of poor or uncertain market information and/or poor implementation. V_m represents the line of total profits (losses) for the move up until T_i, where the action is withdrawn (because of continued losses). In this case the second firm never enters, but instead allows the first mover to absorb the loss. Indeed, imitation by the second firm may make matters worse for both firms. Thus, the strategy for the second firm is to delay moving until it is clear that the first move will be profitable.

Next, consider Case 2, wherein the first move generates profits but only after an initial period of market uncertainty during which the move generates losses. For example, customers may finally realize that a price cut does not mean inferior quality. V_m represents the line of total profits for the first mover, assuming that there is no competitive reaction (including initial losses). The total potential profit from the event is approximated by the line b(t), which is assumed to be constant over time. Note that it takes time for any move to realize its full potential. At time T_i the fast second firm moves and begins to erode some of the profits the first mover intended to capture.[1] The effect of this competition is shown on V_i. The distance between V_m and V_i is the profits realized by the imitator, assuming that the total profit pool is not shrunk by competition. The distance under V_i is what remains for the first mover (including initial losses). In this instance the fast second imitator can potentially outperform the first mover. Suppose further, however, that another imitator delays considerably but finally imitates at T_{ii}. This imitator will capture a much smaller share of the total profits, the distance between V_m and V_{ii}. According to this model, by waiting until the move proves to be profitable but still acting ahead of other rivals, the fast second can potentially outperform the first mover and the late imitator.

As Figure 7.1 suggests, the fast second strategy may well be the prime strategy given ease of imitation. Two very important dimensions of the fast second strategy are move *timing* and *order*. Move timing concerns the amount of time it takes for a firm to respond to the first mover's action. Move order, on the other hand, reflects the temporal rank position of a responder relative to the first mover and other responders.

The timing and order of moves by rivals can be directly linked to the manner by which firms gain advantage. For example, the

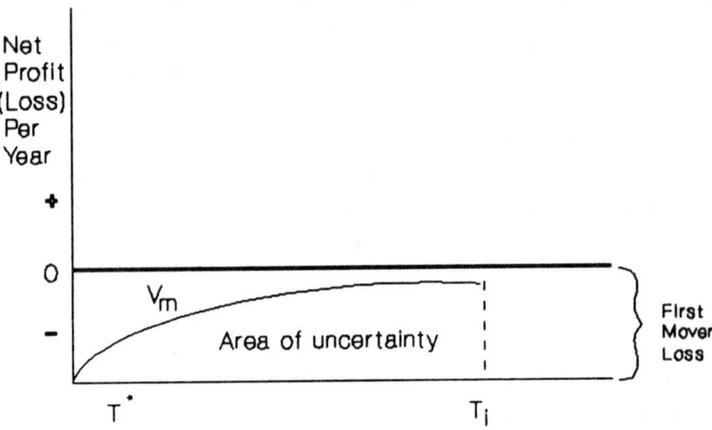

First mover loss without imitation when move is unsuccessful.

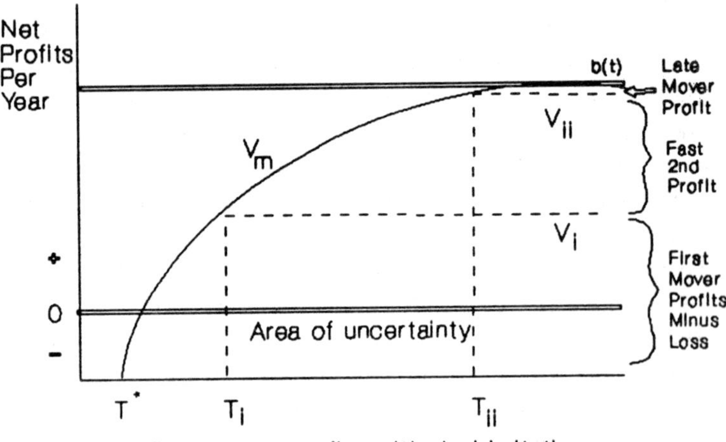

First mover profits with rival imitation.

Figure 7.1. Move-Order Scenarios

extent to which a first mover can benefit from learning curve effects relative to later movers can be observed by the timing of a rival's responses. Since learning can occur only over time, the faster a rival responds, the less the relative learning advantage of the first mover over the fast second. In this regard, fast second firms may also exploit learning curve effects relative to other late moving rivals. Moreover, the timing of rival responses to a first move may well reflect the effectiveness of the first mover's manipulation of other key variables that may block or impede response, such as research and development, preemption of scarce resources, and customer switching costs. By contrast, a speedy response by a fast second may well reflect both an ineffective manipulation of these resources and ease of imitation.

Move order, although clearly related to timing, emphasizes the notion of moving ahead of rivals, that is, moving second or third in the sequence of responders, versus moving later. For all of the same reasons that the first mover may benefit relative to late movers, fast seconds should be better off than late movers. For example, in the case where a first mover's price cut results in an increased market share at the expense of rivals, the fast second will benefit relative to late movers. Move order may be especially important in the resolution of market uncertainty and when there are shifts in customer needs. As shown in Figure 7.1, a firm that is able to move ahead of rivals, when the market becomes more certain or when customer needs have stabilized, probably lowers its level of risk, but it still enjoys the benefits relative both to first movers who move with uncertainty, and to very late movers who have missed the opportunity.

Based on the model presented in Case 2 of Figure 7.1 and the above arguments, the fundamental hypothesis in this chapter is that in rivalry involving relatively easy-to-imitate moves, first movers and fast early movers emphasizing a fast second strategy will outperform slower and later imitators. The model also includes a number of control variables: the types of moves under consideration, industry concentration, and the capabilities of the moving firm. We can now discuss each of these control variables.

First, the performance implications of the fast second strategy may well depend on the type of move undertaken by the first moving firm. In rivalry, the key dimension of move type is its ease of imitation, in that the fast second strategy will result in better performance when moves can be quickly imitated. We controlled for ease of imitation largely by selecting a sample of moves that could be easily imitated, as discussed in more detail below. To further control for the influence of ease of imitation in the model, the authors classified moves into the two categories, strategic and tactical, based on the definitions provided in Chapter 4. Recall that tactical moves, such as price changes and advertising, involve commitments of relatively few resources; strategic moves involve commitments of significantly greater resources. It follows from this distinction that tactical moves requiring fewer resources will be easier to imitate than strategic moves requiring greater resources.

In addition to move type, the model controls for several other variables, which are thought to affect firm performance and have commonly been included in previous industrial organization and strategy studies. For example, industrial organization theory suggests that the degree of seller concentration is one of the most important determinants of firm performance (Scherer & Ross, 1990). The most popular measure of concentration is the Herfindahl-Hirschman index, which is calculated by summing the square of each firm's market share (Hirschman, 1964). This index, which is included as a control variable, is based on the degree of competition faced by each airline in the specific geographic markets it serves.

Two firm-specific factors are also commonly included in studies of firm performance and, in particular, may impact the fast second-performance relationship. These factors are firm size and debt level. Regarding size, larger firms will be more capable of carrying out the fast second strategy than smaller firms. Scherer and Ross describe the case in which a large firm, with an extensive distribution system and sales network, waits for the innovator to move first and remove the market uncertainty, at which point the large firm can quickly penetrate the market and erode the first mover's profits. On the other hand, a small firm may not have the necessary resources to quickly and effectively respond to a rival's initiatives.

Another firm-specific variable that may influence the fast second-performance relationship is the debt level of the firm. Firms with high levels of debt may be unable to generate the resources to act swiftly (Bourgeois, 1981). In addition, organizations with significant debt may be risk adverse (Jensen & Meckling, 1976). High levels of debt make the firm vulnerable to bankruptcy, and executives might avoid risky actions that could put the firm over the edge. When faced with the uncertainty of moving early, a firm with high debt levels may be forced to be conservative and move only when uncertainty is totally reduced (Bowman, 1980; 1982; Greenhalgh, 1983).

In summary, we will test the effects of move time and order on performance in competitive rivalry involving ease of imitation. We will include the types of moves undertaken (strategic/tactical), market concentration, firm size, and firm debt levels as control variables; and we will compare the results of these tests to the results of studies involving more difficult-to-imitate moves from other industries.

Measures

There are a number of important measurement issues associated with testing the relationship between move timing or move order and performance. These issues include the identification and selection of easy-to-imitate moves, the appropriate unit of analysis for testing performance hypotheses, and the definitions and measurement of variables. We discuss these issues in turn.

Ease of Imitation

Recall from the descriptions of the airline study in Chapter 2 that a total of 191 competitive interactions were identified.

These 191 interactions included 191 first moves and 418 competitive responses. Table 2.2 from Chapter 2 provides a list of the different moves included in this sample; the various actions and responses were composed of 16 different types of moves, including service improvements, price cuts, price increases, new advertising campaigns, and so on. Given the many different types of moves in this sample, meaningful statistical analysis of any one single category is not possible because of a limited number of observations. Controlling for the key dimension of ease of imitation provides an acceptable alternative. Moves that can be easily imitated would carry swift response times. The very fast average response time of *11.7 days* per first move in the airline sample emphasizes the relative ease of imitation of these moves. Because the method was based on first selecting responses and then tracing back to the original moves, actions that elicited no response are not included in the sample. Such moves are very difficult to code as data in any systematic and unbiased fashion. Moreover, moves that elicited no response are either more difficult-to-imitate or more likely to be ineffectual in that they attract no responses. Thus the sample of moves under consideration can be considered easy-to-imitate.

Unit of Analysis

As noted in Chapter 2, utilizing a series of dynamic competitive interactions as the unit of analysis creates a number of important measurement issues. Concerning performance, a specific move/response interaction will generally occur over a period of days, while performance data is only publicly available on an annual basis. For example, competitive interaction might occur in January, while performance measures are only available for year-end. The authors overcame this problem by calculating average annual move time and order scores for each airline in the sample which then match the unit of analysis for the performance data. This unit of analysis is both statistically and conceptually appropriate. Statistically, within any given year, the variance for the time and order measures between organizations is significantly greater than the variation within organizations. Therefore, using average year-end response scores takes into account the interdependence inherent in a single firm's competitive moves within a given year (Glick & Roberts, 1984). The alternative to this procedure would be to use each competitive event as a unit of analysis. However, annual performance data would then have to be duplicated to match with each event of a given year. While this would significantly add to the number of cases, "all reported significant tests would be overly liberal" (Glick & Roberts, p. 725). Conceptually, this approach is consistent with Porter's (1980) notion of competitive profiles, which portray a pattern of the firm's competitive behavior over time and, according to Porter, are useful predictors of future competitive behaviors. Thus, the hypotheses will be tested with yearly average move scores, arguably a conservative approach.

Consistent with the above arguments, a pooled cross-section/time series timing and order data set was constructed from the 191 actions and their associated 418 responses over the 8-year period. For our purposes, an observation consists of a firm's actual move/response activity in a given year. Since some firms did not move or respond during a given year, the final data set contains 104 observations.[2] Observations are thus averages of each firm's move/response activity over the year or, in statistical parlance, "grouped data." This method gives rise to heteroscedasticity, with uneven variances a function of the number of moves over which the observation is averaged. The appropriate estimation technique in this instance is weighted-least-squares (Maddala, 1977, p. 268). A heuristic explanation of this technique is that observations averaged across greater number of moves are weighted in the regression more heavily than those based on fewer moves. The specific procedures and definitions for each variable are as follows.

Variable Definitions

Type of Moves. Although the rapid response time of the sample of moves examined suggests relative ease of imitation, additional insights may be obtained by classifying the moves into two subcategories: strategic versus tactical. As discussed earlier in Chapter 4, strategic actions involve significant commitments of specific resources that are difficult both to implement and to reverse once implemented; tactical actions involve fewer commitments of more general resources. Experts were given a list of moves and asked to distinguish strategic actions from tactical actions. The distinction between strategic and tactical proved useful in differentiating moves according to ease of imitation. For example, the responses to tactical actions averaged 8.44 days, whereas responses to strategic actions averaged 34.44 days; this difference was statistically significant.

Based on the above classification, the proportion of strategic moves versus tactical moves was measured for each organization, for each year. Specifically, the number of times a firm undertook strategic moves in a given year was divided by the total number of moves it made, to provide a percentage of strategic actions (labeled strategic actions). For example, if a firm undertook 10 moves in a year and 3 of these moves were considered to be strategic, then the score would be .30. Since the inverse of strategic is tactical, the tactical score would automatically be .70.

Move Time. This was measured by the amount of time in days it took a firm (as reported by Aviation Daily) to respond to a competitor's first move. This measure is very similar to the measure of response lag described in Chapter 2, the difference being that it also includes the first movers scored as 0. The amount of time was measured by the temporal difference between the dates that a specific competitive move and a response were reported in *Aviation Daily*. For example, if Delta altered its fare structure on December 4 in response to American's December 1 fare cut, Delta's move time would be 3, while the first move would be given a move time of 0. As noted above, a firm's average move time was used in the current research. It was calculated by averaging the amount of time it took a given airline to move or react in each event for each year. Thus, if United Airlines undertook four moves in 1982 and at intervals of 0, 10, 14, and 16 days, its average move time for 1982 would be 10 days.

Move Order. This was measured by the rank position in time of the moving firm among all movers involved in a specific event. This measure is very similar to the measure of response order described in Chapter 2, the difference being that it also includes the first movers scored as 1. A firm's average move order was utilized for the current research. It was calculated by averaging each airline's actual rank position in the order of movers for each event, for each year. For example, if Delta Airlines proceeded to take five moves in 1985 and its order in these moves was 1st, 2nd, 2nd, 1st, and 4th among a group of rivals, its average move order for 1985 would be 2nd.

Herfindahl-Hirschman Index. This index is the most common measure of seller concentration; it reflects both the number of competitors in an industry and their inequality (Hirschman, 1964). When a specific industry is dominated by only one firm, the index will equal 1. The value will decline as the number of competitors increases (N), and it also decreases as the disparity in size among competitors increases. By squaring the market shares, the value of larger firms is weighted more heavily. However, for the index to be meaningful, market shares must be calculated across relevant markets in which firms actually compete with one another. Accordingly, this research calculated the index for disaggregated geographic markets and averaged these scores across the markets in which each airline competes.

Measures of organizational size and debt level were obtained for each participating airline, for each year, from *Air Carrier Financial Statistics*. Organizational size was measured by total operating revenue for each airline, for each year. Total debt level was inferred by total interest expense divided by total operating revenues. As the total level of organizational debt increases in a firm, interest expense as a percentage of total revenue will also increase.

Table 7.1 Means, Standard Deviations, and Correlations of All Variables (Airline Study) (non-log values)

Variable	*Mean*	*Standard Deviation*	*1*	*2*	*3*	*4*	*5*	*6*	*7*
1. Move Time	11.51	16.44							
2. Move Order	2.05	1.82	.35***						
3. Size[a]	1.87	1.56	−.15⁺	−.23**					
4. Strategic Action[b]	13.00%	0.21	.17*	−.26**	−.04				
5. Debt Level	.004	.003	.11	−.09	.22**	−.16*			
6. Herfindahl–Hirschman	.26	.08	.00	.02	.01	.16*	.14		
5. Net Income as a Percentage of Total Operating Revenue	−.012	.02	.13⁺	.07	.18*	.03	.04	.44***	
6. Net Income as a Percentage of Total Revenue Passenger Miles	−.0170	.15	.12*	−.06	.22**	.07	−.02	.36***	.68***

⁺$p<.10$
*$p<.05$
**$p<.01$
***$p<.001$
$n = 104$
[a] = Total revenue passenger miles in millions of passenger miles.
[b] = Proportion of strategic moves versus tactical moves.

Performance. This was measured by two indices of net income: net income before tax as a percentage of total operating airline revenue, and net income before tax as a percentage of total revenue passenger miles. These measures were obtained for each airline, for each year, from the *Air Carrier Financial Statistics.*

Results

Table 7.1 reports the means, standard deviations, and correlations among the major variables in this study. Regression

Table 7.2 Weighted Least Squared Regression Results of Timing and Order on Airline Performance (standardized β coefficients reported: standard errors in parentheses)

	Net Income Percent of Sales	*Net Income Percent of Revenue Passenger Miles*
Size[a,b]	6.274***	8.384***
	(1.407)	(1.306)
Strategic Actions[a,c]	-.027	-.085
	(.132)	(.123)
Herfindahl-Hirschman	2.128***	1.948***
	(.496)	(1.421)
Debt Level	.069	-.252
	(.166)	(.154)
Move Timing[a]	.755**	.853**
	(.263)	(.243)
Move Order[a]	-.175+	-.304*
	(.133)	(.123)
R^2	.35	.44
F-Test	7.375***	10.822***

one-tailed t-test
+*p*<.10
**p*<.05
***p*<.01
[a] = Natural log values
[b] = Total revenue passenger miles in millions of passenger miles
[c] = Proportion of strategic moves versus tactical moves
n = 104

analyses were employed to investigate the influence of timing and order on performance. As discussed in the method section, a weighted-least-squares method was employed to correct for heteroscedasticity due to the grouping of moves by organization within a given year (Maddala, 1977). In addition, initial analysis of residuals indicated a curvilinear relationship, and a log-linear model (with natural log transformations) best fit the data.[3]

The regression results are similar for both measures of performance and are reported in Table 7.2. As can be observed, the overall models and a number of the coefficients are statistically significant. First, consider the control variables. As one would expect, organization size and the Herfindahl-Hirschman index are positively related to performance. Thus, large airlines and airlines facing fewer competitors outperform small airlines and airlines that face greater competition. Type of move and debt level were not related to performance.

Next, consider the main effects of move timing and order on performance. Move timing is positively related to performance for both net income before tax as a percentage of total operating airline revenue ($\beta = .755$; $p<.01$) and net income before tax as a percentage of total revenue passenger miles ($\beta = .853$; $p<.001$). This suggests that, on average, slow-moving airlines outperform fast-moving airlines.

However, move order is negatively related to performance for both net income before tax as a percentage of total operating airline revenue ($\beta = -.175$; $p<.10$) and net income before tax as a percentage of total revenue passenger miles ($\beta = -.304$; $p<.05$). This suggests that airlines who move earlier do better than those who are later in the order. Also important, these relationships hold after controlling for the influence of move type and the other environmental and organizational factors.

In addition, there was no significant interaction between time and order on performance; nor were there any significant interactions between the environmental and organizational variables and time and order on performance (analysis not shown). Thus, the research shows that, holding timing and the other variables constant, early movers outperform late movers; and in contrast, holding order and the other variables constant, slow movers outperform fast movers.

The primary question of interest is whether a firm that waits in the wings and moves second can do as well or better than the first mover in competitive rivalry. The answer to this question is unclear from just examining the signs of the timing and order coefficients. That is, the second moving firm in comparison to the first moving firm will necessarily be lower on the order (negative effect on performance) but slower (positive effect on performance). Which of these two effects is likely to dominate?

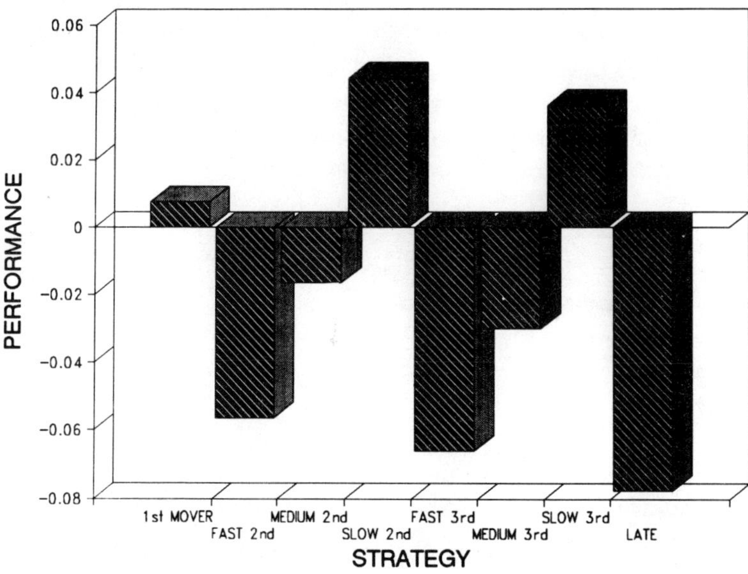

Figure 7.2. Move Order, Speed, and Performance

To shed additional light on these opposite effects, performance implications of a number of representative average time/ order strategies were calculated. More specifically, eight profile strategies were chosen: average first mover; average fast, medium, and slow second; average fast, medium, and slow third; and average late mover. These strategic profiles were selected to portray the potential range of alternative move behaviors available to firms. For second and third movers, the fast, medium, and slow times were based on sample characteristics (fast = the top 10th percentile; medium = the 50th percentile; and slow = the bottom 90th percentile). For example, the range of timing values associated with an average move order of second was 1 day to 51 days with fast, medium, and slow scores of 1.67, 4.3, and 17 days, respectively. Performance implications of the eight profile strategies were then generated by plugging appropriate values for order and time into the regression equation. The results are portrayed in Figure 7.2.

It can be observed that under certain conditions, second movers can outperform first movers. However, the slow second does well, while the fast second does poorly. Slow third firms also do relatively well, while fast thirds do badly. Finally, in accordance with expectations, late firms have the lowest performance.

Discussion and Integration

The purpose of this chapter was to examine the performance consequences of move timing and order in competitive rivalry. Although it was hypothesized that early and fast movers would outperform slow and late movers, the results suggest an intriguing alternative strategy: the slow second strategy. Also important, the relationship between timing and order as they influence performance was not affected by the number of competitors, the type of move undertaken, or the size and debt of the moving firm.

Although the results may seem paradoxical at first glance, there is a logical interpretation that has important implications for managers. In competitive rivalry involving easy-to-imitate moves, it is better to be one of the first firms pursuing the initiative as opposed to one of the last. However, it is beneficial to delay in responding if, in the process, one does not slip down in the order. Waiting longer to respond will presumably allow more time for market uncertainty to clear and will also allow for a more appropriate action. Monitoring competitors is therefore of paramount importance. In short, a firm must assess whether it can afford the luxury of waiting, or whether its delaying will allow other firms to beat it to the punch.

Of course, achieving the optimal trade-off between time and order, as represented by the slow second strategy, is probably quite difficult in practice. When a firm delays its response, other firms may well move more quickly and the delaying firm may find itself in the greatly flawed "late" position. Thus, in the presence of a rival's action, a firm may have to deliberately formulate the best response but carefully anticipate responses

Table 7.3 The Relationship Between Competitive Moves and Performance Among High-Technology Firms

	*Performance**			
Types of Moves	*Sales Growth*	*Return on Sales*	*Return on Assets*	*Overall Performance*
Cutting Price	2.86	3.00	3.29	11.75
Advertising	3.43	3.00	2.71	12.57
Introducing New Product	4.20	3.80	3.80	15.80
Altering R&D	5.00	5.00	3.80	20.00
Improving Product Quality	4.00	3.80	3.80	15.40
	$F = 2.58$	$F = 1.385$	$F = 1.846$	$F = 2.924$
	$p<.10$	N.S.	N.S.	$p<.10$

N.S. = Not Significant
* 1 to 5 scale, with 1 being the lowest performance.

by other rivals. Intimate knowledge of rivals' capabilities and proclivities can obviously pay great dividends.

Recall that this research employed average annual move time and order measures; thus, the results pertain more to an airline's average competitive behavior in a given year than to its behavior in any one competitive event. In this regard, the slow second strategy may be thought of as an ideal strategy profile for rivalry.

The results of the airline study should be considered preliminary and exploratory. The research could be extended through the study of moves that are more difficult-to-imitate. Table 4.4 from Chapter 4 suggests that the moves identified in the electrical-manufacturing and high-technology studies are much more difficult-to-imitate. For example, the response time to strategic actions in the electrical manufacturing study averaged 271 days and in the high technology study 540 days. This is in contrast to the average response time to strategic actions in the airline study of 34 days. Recall that in the airline study the type of move had no effect on performance (Table 7.2). However, as revealed in Table 7.3, the type of move does have some impact on performance in the high-technology study. Also important,

Table 7.4 Correlations Between Move Timing and Performance Among High-Technology and Electrical-Manufacturing Firms

High-Technology Firms	*Sales Growth*	*Return on Sales*	*Return on Assets*	*Overall Performance*
Pearson Correlation	–.32	–.33	–.54	–.38
Number of Firms	25	25	24	25
Significance Level	.06	.05	.01	.03
Electrical-Manufacturing Firms	*Return Growth*	*Return on Sales*		
Pearson Correlation	–.36	–.32		
Number of Firms	22	22		
Significance Level	.05	.09		

the types of moves that seem to have the longest response times (e.g., introducing new products and altering R&D) are associated with the highest performance. Although very preliminary, these results suggest that ease of move imitation is a key variable in rivalry. In combination, the results suggests that there is a continuum of moves that vary in the degree to which they can be duplicated by rivals, and that the response times associated with each move is a viable proxy for ease of imitation. Future research should focus attention on other characteristics of move imitation.

Recall also that in the airline study the relationship between move timing and performance was positive, suggesting the slow second strategy. However, as suggested in Table 7.4, in both the high-technology study and the electrical-manufacturing study the correlations between move timing and performance are negative. Again, a key distinction between the studies is the ease with which moves can be imitated. Thus, when moves can be readily imitated, firms should move slowly but strive to be ahead of competitors. In contrast, when moves cannot be easily imitated, firms should strive to respond as quickly as possible. This is, of course, assuming that a response is necessary. Future research should identify the conditions under which response time is both positively and negatively related to performance.

Alternative performance measures should be examined in future research. In particular, it would be interesting to utilize performance measures that would more precisely match the specific moves of firms. One approach would be to link the specific lower-order moves of firms with the stock market reactions to those moves. The timing and order of moves could also be brought into the model. For example, timing of rival responses could be correlated with the stock market impacts of the first move. However, jockeying for position with lower-order moves is often a daily occurrence. Thus, there may be significant overlap between effects of first moves and the impacts of the reactions of rivals on stock market values. Relatedly, determining the window for measuring effects—1 day, 7 days, or 30 days—when there are multiple events over the same period would be problematic. For example, the 1-day impact of a first move could be easily offset by rivals' responses the very next day. Accordingly, it may be very difficult to properly measure the effects of move timing and order on stock market data for lower-order moves. Nonetheless, such an effort might be fruitful in a less rivalrous setting, where delays in responses are more common.

In summary, although scope remains for future extensions of the research, the present study has provided an important contribution to our understanding of competitive rivalry. This research not only provides the first systematic empirical tests of the value of timing and order in rivalry but also subjects the wealth of theory on first mover advantages and fast second strategies to further empirical verification. Controlling for key firm and industry factors, the results provide evidence that competitive timing and order have significant impacts on firm performance. In particular, this research improves our understanding of how firms should behave in everyday competition where rivals can easily imitate. As noted previously, Porter (1990) has argued that it is in this context that competitive advantage is primarily built. In addition, the results from the high technology study expand our knowledge to settings involving more difficult-to-imitate actions. Additional research in this area would help provide a more complete and balanced picture of the performance consequences of different competitive behaviors.

Notes

1. This is assuming ease of imitation, low switching costs, and that the action is equal or more appropriate to the market than the first move.

2. Overall, there were 14 observations of 1 move in a year, 22 observations of 2 moves in a year, 10 observations of 3 moves, 14 observations of 4 moves, 4 observations of 5 moves, 11 observations of 6 moves, 6 observations of 7 moves, 2 observations of 8 moves, 3 observations of 9 moves, 1 observation of 12 moves, 3 observations of 13 moves, 2 observations of 14 moves, 6 observations of 15 moves, 3 observations of 17 moves, and 1 observation of 19 moves in a year.

3. The results did not differ substantially for a regression equation in which the normal values of timing and order were run along with a squared term for each. Both the normal values and the squared terms were significant.

8

An Alternative Perspective on Rivalry: Avoiding Wars With Competitors

THE preceding chapters have focused on firm rivalry and advantage: how to take actions and responses that will result in superior profits over rivals. The emphasis has been on outcompeting rivals, seizing opportunities to lead the industry by introducing marketing campaigns, pricing initiatives, or technologically superior products designed specifically to attract market share from competitors, increase revenues, and ultimately add to the bottom line. Although the specific focus on and investigation of firm actions and responses is novel with regard to this book, the emphasis on outcompeting rivals is clearly the dominant perspective in the strategic management literature.

Indeed, the field of strategic management relies heavily on the metaphor of war to explain competitive interaction among rivals. This reliance is so widespread that it is rarely questioned. For example, a large literature on generic strategies identifies the specific fundamental strategies that will be superior to others (Porter, 1980). It can even be said that the common thread in the strategy literature is an emphasis on warfare or competition and a strong notion that a firm must outcompete its rivals if it wants to be successful and even survive. There are several interrelated propositions incorporated into this metaphor, one of the most important of which is the assumption that when one firm in an industry makes a highly visible competitive move, other firms will respond to it or at least consider responding to it to properly defend their own positions. Another involves surprise or the advantage that results from acting or moving early and ahead of rivals.

This chapter considers a very different and alternative perspective on achieving strong financial performance, which is that a firm may well achieve maximum profits by not competing, or by competing less intensively. More specifically, firms acting collectively with others to limit rivalry may well achieve higher profits for all than would exist if rivalry were intense. The field of industrial organization economics (IO)—which differs from strategic management in terms of a greater focus on an industry level of analysis and an emphasis on society's rather than an individual firm's welfare—has historically stressed the movement toward coordination in oligopolistic industries. A central question in IO is whether a small number of firms dominating an industry will recognize their mutual interdependence and collude in some fashion to achieve above-normal profits. Firms in such industries, while they may be partial to the war metaphor, realize that they may kill each other off if they follow this metaphor to its logical conclusion. In particular, price wars, whereby prices are repeatedly slashed in response to price reductions by competitors, are clearly to be avoided in the best interests of all firms' profits.

The central argument of this chapter is that firms are more likely to recognize their mutual interdependence and lessen the degree of rivalry under certain industry-structural conditions.

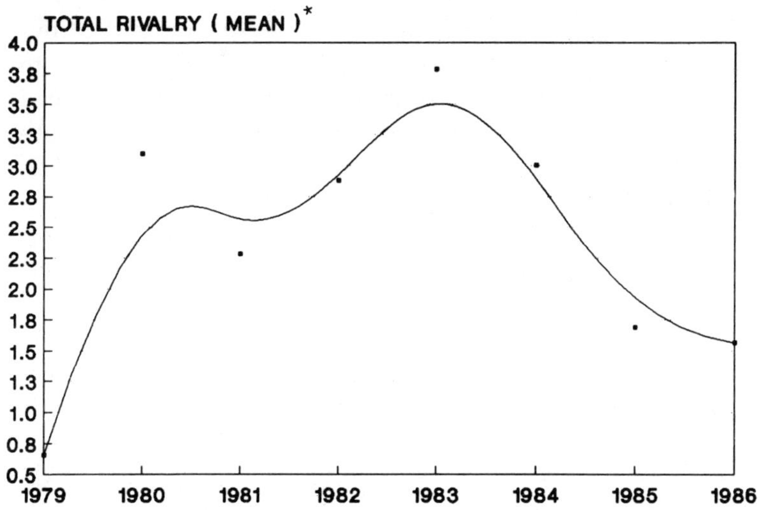

Figure 8.1. Rivalrous Conduct in the Airline Industry

This chapter presents hypotheses regarding the industry-structural conditions that will facilitate less rivalry and greater coordination. Preliminary evidence is presented, based on 8 years of data from the airline study.[1]

Degree of Rivalry

An innovative feature of the chapter is our measure of industry rivalry. More specifically, the degree of rivalry is measured by the average number of actions and responses each competitor undertakes in a given year. When the average number of actions and reactions a firm undertakes is high, rivalry will be high; when the number is low, industry rivalry will be lower and it is reasonable to conclude that there is greater implicit coordination. Figure 8.1 portrays the degree of rivalry in the airline industry over 8 years. Note that the degree of rivalry is low in 1979, perhaps indicating a slowness in initially responding to new freedoms from deregulation. The number of actions accelerates greatly in the subsequent years, with the greatest number in 1983, falls in 1984 and is much lower in 1985 and 1986. It is also worth noting that when the average number of actions and reactions for each firm in the industry is high, both the speed of competitive response to each action and the number of responders to each action are high. Next, consider the relationship between the degree of rivalry and performance.

Degree of Rivalry as a Determinant of Performance

The perspective that coordination of firms' actions can enhance profits is perhaps most prominent in the antitrust literature. As discussed in more detail by Sullivan (1977), formal collusion, such as overt agreements to fix prices at certain levels or to divvy up markets, has long been illegal in the United States, dating back to the 1890 Sherman Act. That there have nonetheless been salient examples of firms engaging in such conduct underscores the importance attached to coordination in enhancing firm performance. For example, the informal agreements about the distribution of market share that existed for decades in several large industries in the United States, such as the electric utilities industry, are viewed as very rational by some executives in these industries, and some of those executives have gone to great lengths to bolster and sustain the agreements. For instance, meetings establishing these agreements among executives from several firms in the electric utilities industry occurred in major American cities for several years during the 1940s and 1950s, and the site for each meeting was chosen to coincide with various phases of the moon so as to confuse Justice Department investigators seeking to prove that collusion among the firms existed. Indeed, many years elapsed before these investigators established the relationship between the cycles of the moon and the scheduling of these meetings.

Sometimes executives are found to be in blatant violation of antitrust laws, as happened in the electric utilities industry during the 1950s, when several executives were fined and/or sent to jail. One of the best-known recent examples occurred when Robert Crandall, president of American Airlines, talked on the telephone to Howard Putnam, chairman of Braniff International Corporation, about the competitive battle then raging in 1982 between American and Braniff on a number of routes served out of the Dallas/Fort Worth Airport. Putnam taped this conversation and turned the tape over to the Justice Department. An excerpt from this taped conversation follows:

Crandall: "I think it's dumb as hell for crissakes, all right, to sit here and pound the [expletive] out of each other and neither of us making a [expletive] dime."

Putnam: "But . . . I can't just sit here and allow you to bury us without giving our best effort . . . Do you have a suggestion for me?"

Crandall: "Yes, I have a suggestion for you. Raise your [expletive] fares 20 percent. I'll raise mine the next morning. . . . You'll make more money, and I will, too."

Putnam: "We can't talk about pricing."

Crandall: "Oh [expletive], Howard, we can talk about any [expletive] thing we want to talk about."

While such overt agreements to restrict competition are clearly illegal, presumably relatively uncommon, and not to be encouraged, antitrust precedents allow for a range of less overt "tacit" coordination and "conscious parallelism" activity. For example, as discussed in more detail by Scherer and Ross (1990), firms may charge the same prices and change prices together over time, but as long as there is no overt agreement to do so, such activity will not generally be judged illegal. Also, all firms in an industry can maintain high prices relative to costs, thereby earning handsome profits; again, absent a formal agreement, such activity is *not* illegal.

Although the implications of such activity are profound, the actual study of the dynamics of competitive interaction in the strategy area has been very limited, especially in the area of

Table 8.1 Payoffs to Two Firms in Price Game

	Firm B's Price	
Firm A's Price	*High*	*Low*
High	111,111	57,122
Low	12,257	95,95

coordination. One study of note is that completed by Richard Bettis and David Weeks (1987), which examined the competitive moves of Kodak and Polaroid in the instant photography industry between January 14, 1976, and November 23, 1977. Using the game-theoretic formulation of the Prisoners' Dilemma in a two-by-two matrix (two competitors can either fight or seek détente with one another), Bettis and Weeks showed that fighting led to low profits for both Kodak and Polaroid, while having one firm in a fighting mode as the other sought détente, resulted in an unstable situation. Only détente on the part of both Kodak and Polaroid led to moderate profits. The message of this study seems to be that fighting hurts both firms, and that détente is preferable.

A simple illustration of this game-theoretic formulation can be used to highlight the fundamental issue facing a small number of firms in an industry. With reference to Table 8.1, let us assume that there are only two firms, each with a choice of a high or low price. Payoffs to each firm are a function of the prices each of them charge. If both Firm A and Firm B charge a high price, the payoff for each of them would be identical (111,111), assuming that everything else is equal. Similarly, if each firm charged a low price, the payoff for each firm would again be identical (95, 95) but lower than in the first instance (95, 95) simply because of the price asked. However, if one firm sets a low price while the other uses a high price, the firm with the low price will have a higher payoff because of increased sales (12,257). The payoff (95, 95) is the Nash equilibrium to this game, representing the best each can do given the action of the

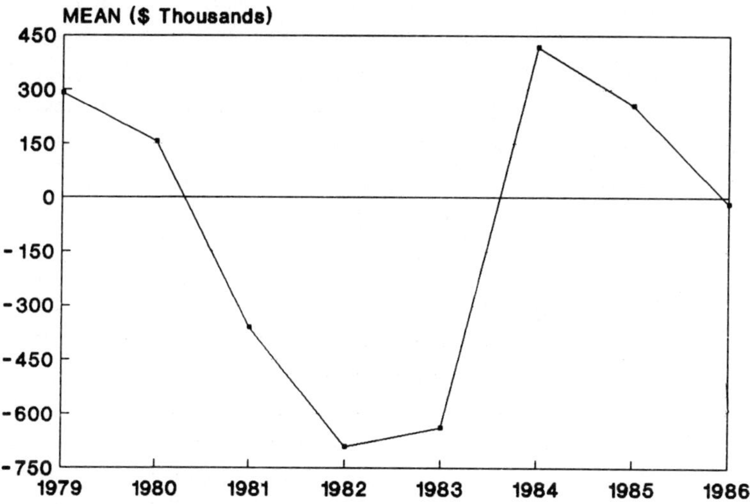

Figure 8.2. Airline Industry Profit

other. It can also be seen as a conservative "cut your losses" type of solution, or more formally as a "maximin."

The challenge for both firms is to achieve the superior payoffs that are a function of the less intense competitive rivalry, that is, both set the higher prices. This example illustrates that the individual pricing strategy each firm pursues is not nearly as important as coordinating prices to achieve the optimal outcome for both firms. Our first hypothesis in this chapter, then, is that less intense industry rivalry will result in a higher level of industry profits.

Figure 8.2 shows that indeed this is the case for the airline industry during the 8-year period of study. The data generally support the first hypothesis, as profits are relatively high in 1979 when rivalry was low, profits are very weak in 1982 and 1983 when rivalry was most intense, and profits rebound in 1984 to 1986 in accordance with reduced rivalry. Other measures of financial performance and intensity of rivalry show similar results.

Industrial Structural Determinants of Rivalry

The degree of rivalry among firms in an industry has long been viewed in industrial organization as largely a function of key structural variables (Scherer & Ross, 1990). These dimensions include industry concentration, strength of industry demand, and homogeneity of firms. Each will be discussed in turn.

Number of Competitors

A long-standing tenet of industrial organization economics is that lower industry concentration will result in greater rivalry. As more firms compete in a market, the degree of rivalry will become more intense. With more firms, the chances are greater that any one maverick firm will set off a fierce competitive skirmish. Also, with additional firms coordination or tacit collusion becomes more difficult, as a greater number of firms increases the probabilities that the firms will have different notions about what price levels will maximize profits. As discussed by Williamson (1965), a major effect of adding more firms is that the number of two-way communication channels over which coordination must occur increases exponentially. For example, with two firms there is only 1 communication channel, with three firms there are 2 channels, with four firms there are 6 channels, and with five firms there are 10. The presence of five firms rather than two results in a situation in which 10 times as many communication channels need to be maintained, with a breakdown in any one of these most likely destroying coordination efforts for the entire industry.[2] A study by Fraas and Greer (1977) of explicit as well as tacit price collusion revealed strong support for the notion that coordination is more difficult with a greater number of firms in an industry. Our second hypothesis, then, is that the number of competitors in an industry will be positively related to the intensity of rivalry.

The number of competitors was measured by counting the number of major airlines in the U.S. domestic market during

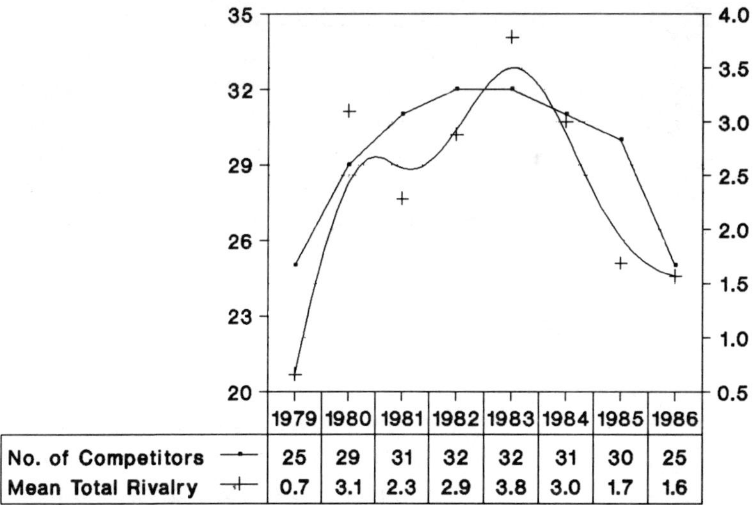

	1979	1980	1981	1982	1983	1984	1985	1986
No. of Competitors	25	29	31	32	32	31	30	25
Mean Total Rivalry	0.7	3.1	2.3	2.9	3.8	3.0	1.7	1.6

Figure 8.3. Number of Competitors and Rivalry

each year. Figure 8.3 reports the relationship between the degree of rivalry and the number of competitors. Clearly, the degree of rivalry for each year is closely related to the number of competitors in the industry for each year. Note that the degree of rivalry is not based on the number of competitors, but on the average number of actions and responses for each year for each firm in the industry. With fewer competitors rivalry declines; with more competitors rivalry increases. The number of competitors declined in the airline industry for many reasons, including mergers and corporate failures or bankruptcies.

Strength of Industry Demand

A growing industry demand will facilitate a "live and let live" attitude on the part of firms. As discussed by Scherer and Ross (1990), in general, a growing pie can encourage stability, as each firm can increase its share of the pie without affecting the other firms' shares. On the other hand, a decrease in demand

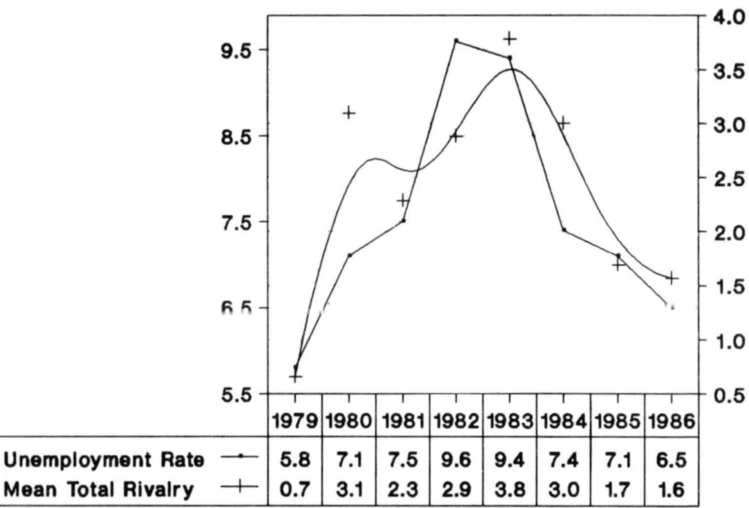

	1979	1980	1981	1982	1983	1984	1985	1986
Unemployment Rate —•—	5.8	7.1	7.5	9.6	9.4	7.4	7.1	6.5
Mean Total Rivalry —+—	0.7	3.1	2.3	2.9	3.8	3.0	1.7	1.6

Figure 8.4. Unemployment Rate and Rivalry

or even a fall in the growth rate, perhaps brought about by an economic downturn, can lead to competitive warfare. Related to industry demand is the degree of capacity utilization in the industry. Firms producing at close to full capacity have little incentive to try to increase output by lowering prices. On the other hand, if firms are faced with excess capacity and idle resources, the temptation is great to lower prices and increase output in an effort to fill excess capacity. As such, a fall in industry demand, where capacity can not easily be reduced, can have a particularly strong effect on increasing rivalry. Our third hypothesis, then, is that strength of industry demand is inversely related to intensity of rivalry.

As a proxy measure of industry demand, we used the unemployment rate for the entire economy and assumed that a high unemployment rate would lessen demand in the consumer-sensitive airline industry. As shown in Figure 8.4, there is general support for this hypothesis because the curves showing the relationship between unemployment and total rivalry are quite similar. During the years when demand was strong, rivalry was low, and vice versa. Other macro indicators, such as the interest rate level, reveal similar patterns.

Homogeneity of Firms

Firms with similar cost structures will find it easier to agree on the same price or similar prices, which, as shown in our game-theoretic example, maximize joint industry profits. Widely varying costs among firms will generally result in stronger rivalry. Also, if firms are more similar on other dimensions such as size, corporate culture, length of time in the industry, and the like, coordination will be easier and rivalry will be less intense.

In particular, the extent to which products are standardized can play an important role. As discussed by Asch and Seneca (1975), if significant product differentiation exists so that each firm's product differs markedly from that of other firms, coordination is more difficult. For example, if a firm incurs significant costs to produce a very high quality product, that firm would look for a relatively high prevailing price, as opposed to a low-cost, low-quality producer who would perhaps push for a lower industry price. This is consistent with the work of Caves and Porter (1977) on strategic group influences on rivalry. They found that rivalry is more intense between rather than within groups. It follows that if distinctions between strategic groups are not pronounced, the industry as a whole will be likely to coordinate actions to the benefit of all. Thus, if factors such as cost position, degree of product differentiation, size, and the like are relatively similar across firms in an industry, we would expect less rivalrous conduct. Thus we hypothesize that homogeneity of firms will be negatively related to intensity of rivalry.

As our measure of firm homogeneity, we employed the coefficient of variation of promotion costs per unit of output (number of seats filled). The higher the coefficient of variation, the more heterogeneous are the firms, particularly as regards degree of product differentiation, and the greater is the expected

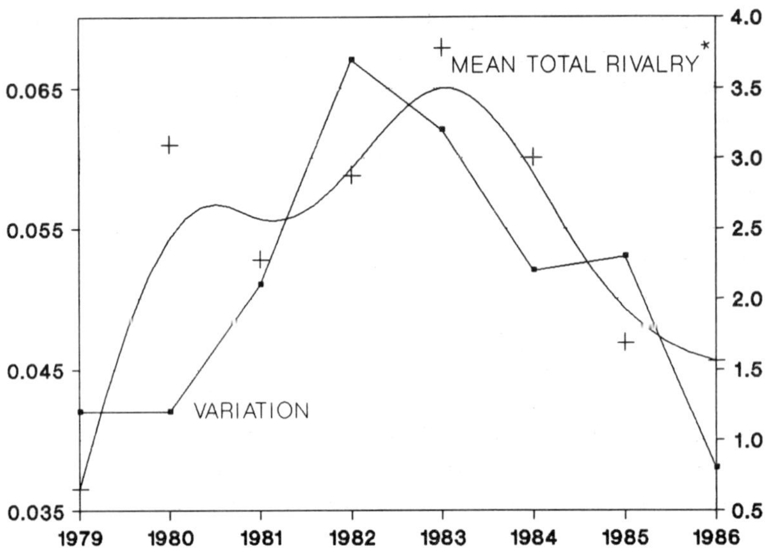

Figure 8.5. Variation of Unit Promotion Cost and Rivalry

rivalry. As shown in Figure 8.5, the curves for the coefficient of variation and the total rivalry parallel one another closely. Other measures, such as service costs, show similar trends.

Managerial Determinants of Rivalry

Although the IO literature has explored a variety of structural factors that influence the degree of rivalry in an industry, little empirical research has been conducted on the role of managerial factors. To successfully coordinate actions across an industry, firms need to be very aware of the actions of others and sensitive to their strategies to facilitate oligopolistic coordination. For example, Porter (1980, 1985) discusses the importance of market signalling—specific actions firms might take, in conjunction with price cuts and other competitive moves, to lessen the possibility of an outbreak of price warfare.

We essentially argue that coordination in the airline industry will be facilitated by a changing of the management guard: from old, experienced, and relatively less educated managers to younger, less experienced, but more educated managers. Airline managers from the regulated period have often been criticized for their strategic complacency. Indeed, notions of the coordination of actions among rivals may not be familiar to old-line airline managers who, under regulation, did not need to worry about competition.

Hambrick and Mason (1984) argued that a manager's age, education, and experience are indicators of an individual's flexibility, capability, and risk-taking propensity. For example, it is generally accepted that as people grow older, they become more inflexible to change and take fewer risks. Younger managers, on the other hand, are more likely to seek growth and attempt actions that would create growth. Hambrick and Mason contended that if top managers have spent their careers in the industry or organization, they will have a limited knowledge base from which to analyze and understand competitors. It is only from such analysis and understanding that managers could develop coordination strategies. Similarly, they argued that the educational level of managers is positively related to organizational innovation or the organization's openness to change. Thus, educated managers will be more likely to recognize their mutual interdependence and act to coordinate rivalry that could ruin profits.

Thus, our hypothesis was that younger, less experienced, and more educated managers would have a greater sense of their competitive interdependence and the advantages of avoiding wars with rivals than would older, more experienced, but less educated managers. The age, experience, and educational levels of the top management team of each airline were obtained from *Dun and Bradstreet Corporate Directory*. Although the results were less clear-cut than those reported above, Figure 8.6 clearly suggests there has been a changing of the guard within the airline industry. In particular, top managers were younger,

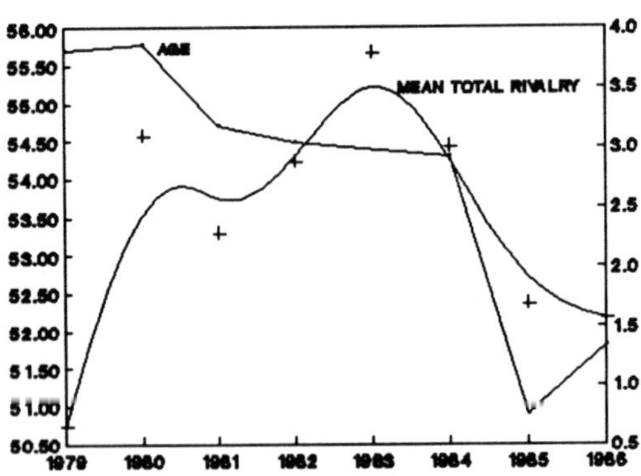

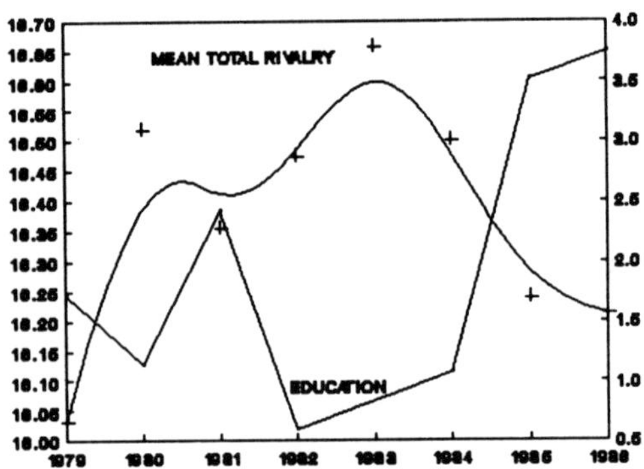

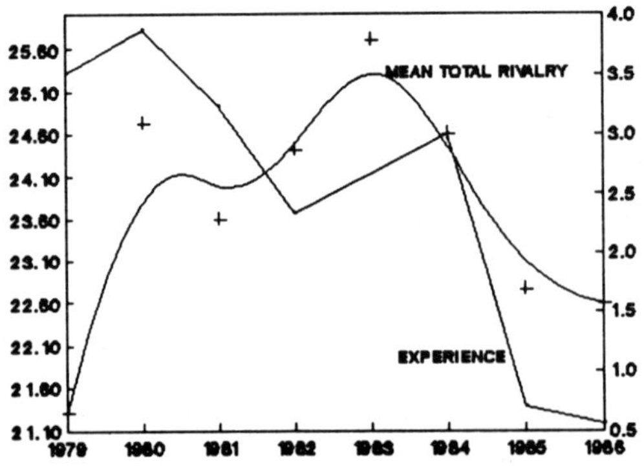

Figure 8.6. Management Characteristics and Rivalry

less experienced, and better educated as rivalry in the industry began to decrease.

Discussion

Using a game-theoretic model similar to that employed by Bettis and Weeks (1987), we similarly observed that avoiding competition results in higher profits for all or most firms in a specific industry. This result suggests that the war metaphor, while it is clearly critical in explaining firm behavior, should be supplemented by one emphasizing coordination among firms in a specific industry. "Live and let live" seems to be a good approach for individual firms that want to survive and prosper. Any action taken by a firm must not only consider the static implications for that firm's costs and revenues, but must also take into account the implications for the degree of industry rivalry. For example, a price cut may increase market share and possible revenues in the short run, but if it brings about a protracted price war such an action may well be unwise.

However, there are several factors that influence the degree to which coordination can be achieved in an industry. As discussed in this chapter, these include the number of competitors in an industry, the state of industry demand as measured by the unemployment rate, homogeneity of costs, and the background of top executives within a specific industry. This study has indicated that all of these factors are related to the intensity of competition. While coordination may be desirable for existing firms in a given industry, it may well be impossible to achieve because of these and related factors. A firm considering entry into or exit from an industry should therefore be aware of factors affecting intensity of rivalry, because future profits may well hang in the balance.

Future Research

The theory and trends presented in this chapter can be extended in a number of directions. First of all, the role of other structural factors in influencing rivalry should be examined. For example, as barriers to entry increase in scope and complexity, coordination among existing firms should become easier. As discussed by Scherer and Ross (1990), new entrants typically inject a great deal of rivalry into an industry. Such firms may come in with low prices in an effort to attract customers from existing firms. Also, a new firm may not be familiar with the established signalling and other communication mechanisms to bring about tacit collusion. Further, new entrants frequently increase the degree of industry capacity and heterogeneity, which, as discussed below, also tend to accelerate the intensity of competition. On the other hand, strong entry barriers increase industry stability and can result in lower rivalry, in that firms can more easily engage in long-term, mutually beneficial actions if they are confident that the same set of players will be in the industry over time.

Also, high industry capacity utilization should result in increased coordination, as firms producing at close to full capacity have little incentive to try to increase output by lowering prices. However, if firms are faced with excess capacity and idle resources, the temptation is great to lower prices and increase output in an effort to soak up excess capacity. These and other structural factors should be studied in greater depth in future research.

The theory could also be enriched and further differentiated from work in industrial organization economics by examination of the effects of additional managerial and strategy variables on rivalry. For example, the role of signalling could be analyzed in greater detail. Also, the impacts of strategy type on coordination may deserve increased attention.

Perhaps most important, future research should concentrate on more rigorous empirical testing of these relationships. The present study is limited by the manner in which hypotheses were tested. No statistical tests were performed, as average scores for each year were used for all variables, thus limiting the number of observations to the number of years studied (8). Future research should build on the methodology developed in this work that allows measurement of industry rivalry. A larger sample suitable for formal statistical methods could be generated by disaggregating an industry into specific markets or by examining multiple industries. In addition, drawing a sample across a number of industries would extend the generalizability of the research.

Conclusion

Despite limitations of the current analysis, the results tend to support the conclusion that coordination or avoiding wars with competitors is related to increased profits for all of the firms involved. In sum, emphasizing only the war or competitive metaphor may be not only misleading but also misguided. The research indicates that firms would do better to avoid war if at all possible. While this possibility may not be realizable in all cases, it should be explored if a firm wants to survive and prosper.

A recent example from the airline industry illustrates both the range of possible coordination activities and the care firms must take not to run afoul of the antitrust laws (Nomani, 1991). Nine major domestic carriers have been charged with price fixing, based on actions taken though computer reservation systems (CRSs). More specifically, critics claim that airlines use CRSs to signal their pricing actions, to better coordinate pricing, and to alert rivals of intended retaliatory action in response to price cuts. For example, according to Nomani:

> Airlines have used future fare reductions to pressure rivals to back off pricing actions they don't favor. The airlines have done this by filing fare cuts with a future effective date in a rival's hub market. The price cuts would be withdrawn if the rival carrier withdrew its own pricing action. (p. B1)

The article went on to state that two firms, Trans World Airlines and Northwest Airlines, had agreed to alter certain of these practices as part of a proposed settlement to remove them from the price fixing lawsuit. Clearly, firms will go to great lengths to derive the benefits from coordination, and the phenomenon certainly deserves further research attention.

Notes

1. The airline industry is particularly suitable for studying firm rivalry and coordination. Following several decades of regulation, which sharply restricted the ability of firms to compete, the industry was deregulated by the Airline Deregulation Act of 1978. So starting this airline study in 1979 helped reduce the number of intervening factors that frequently cloud industry-specific studies.

In addition, the regulated history of this industry resulted in a situation in which a good amount of data was publicly available; airlines must file annual reports that disclose performance, cost, and other data not generally available in many large industries. Also, the industry has a relatively small number of firms, yet provided a rich variation of structural and competitive factors in the years immediately following deregulation.

2. The increasing difficulties of coordination with more firms are analyzed more formally by Osborne (1976).

9

Summarizing and Integrating the Results

THE research described in this book is distinctive in that it analyzes the dynamics of competitive moves and responses by means of a communication-information model through which many significant hypotheses were tested. Several innovative measures of competitive behavior were developed in order to construct comparative response profiles, and these were related to many predictor variables, such as the composition of the top management team and organizational slack. In addition, the research is also distinctive in that triangulation of research methods was emphasized in testing these hypotheses within the scope of three different industries. In this final chapter, we summarize the major findings, using our communication-information model as a vehicle for integrating the results and the discussion of them.

As our model suggests, there are several components of competitive rivalry that can be analytically highlighted: the acting firm or the actor, the action taken, the competitive environment in which it is taken, the responding firm or firms, and the response or responses. Each component other than the types of responses, which were the primary dependent variables in the study, then became the basis for one chapter of the book (Chapters 3 through 6). Chapter 7 focused on the relationship between the timing of the move, irrespective of whether it was the initiating action or the responses of competitors to it, and organizational performance. This analysis was a logical outgrowth of our emphasis on response profiles because we wanted to identify when rapid actions and responses to them were associated positively with organizational performance. Chapter 8 was a rational antithesis to the emphasis on competitive dynamics because it analyzed when and why competitors would cooperate with one another to avoid competition.

In the previous chapters of the book we have described the hypotheses in detail and whether they were confirmed. Overall, there was very strong confirmation of the model and each of its components. In this final chapter we integrate the results by focusing only on those hypotheses that received strong support.

The actual testing of hypotheses began in Chapter 3, where the focus was on the reputations of the acting firms and their reputational indicators that were related to the different types of response or response profiles in the airline industry. Three multiple regression equations were used to relate these independent variables to three measures of competitive response: actual response time in days or response lag, average number of responders, and response imitation. In all three cases there was strong evidence that the reputation of the actor predicts response. Thus, as the reputation of the acting firm's top management team for predictability increased and its aggressiveness decreased, competitors responded more slowly. Also, responses became slower as the acting firm's reputation for either moves of greater magnitude or strategic moves rose, while acting firms with reputations as aggressive price predators elicited faster responses than did their less aggressive counterparts.

Similarly, as the reputation as a market leader of the acting firms rose, so too did the average number of responses. However, as the reputation of the top management teams for predictability and lack of aggressiveness as a price predator rose, the number of responders declined. Also, as the market leader reputation of the acting firms increased, response imitation rose. And response imitation declined as the reputation of the acting firms as strategic players increased.

In Chapter 4 the component of the model that was of interest was the action itself. In this chapter the two aspects of response that were highlighted were response timing and the average number of responders. Clearly, there is strong support for the hypotheses demonstrating that a competitive response is at least partially a function of the action's characteristics.

In the airline study, speed of competitive response or response lag was shown to be related to the magnitude of the action (tactical to strategic), the threat of the action itself (minor to major), and implementation requirements (easy to difficult). More specifically, as magnitude and implementation requirements of an action increased, response time also rose. But as the threat of the action became major, response time declined.

Using the same data base, these three characteristics and scope (affecting few to many competitors) were then regressed against the average number of responders. As expected, as magnitude and implementation requirements increased, the number of responders declined. But the threat of the action was positively related to the average number of responders.

In the electrical-manufacturing study, similar results were obtained. That is, as the degree of radicality of the actions or the degree to which past information was of little, if any, use rose, responses were slower; and actions that were seen as threatening were correlated with faster response times.

In this chapter the formal testing of hypotheses through the use of multiple regression was supplemented by descriptive data, which proved to be very persuasive. In particular, there were clear differences in the average number of days it took firms to respond to strategic and tactical actions, and great variations by type of industry in these averages. In addition, there were clear variations in the response times associated with specific types of moves (for example, cutting prices) and specific types of responses.

Chapter 5 spotlighted the characteristics of the responding firms that could be used to predict competitive response. Four different measures of response were of interest: response timing or lag, response order or a firm's average ranking in a series of responses, response imitation, and response likelihood or a firm's probability of response.

For the airline data four separate regressions were run, using each of these response measures as a dependent variable. Overall, there was strong support for relating the characteristics of the responding firm to response. Thus, as a firm's external orientation rose, so too did its likelihood of response, while response lag and order decreased. Also, structural complexity was negatively related to response likelihood. Structural complexity was also correlated positively to response order. Further, firms led by top management teams with fewer years of industry experience were more likely to respond and to respond earlier than their more experienced counterparts, while firms led by highly educated top management teams were more likely to imitate the action.

Two types of organizational slack were measured in this part of the airline study: absorbed, referring specifically to the slack absorbed in the costs of organization; and unabsorbed, referring chiefly to uncommitted liquid resources. As expected, unabsorbed slack was associated negatively with response imitation. However, the other relationships tended to be either insignificant or in the opposite direction to the predictions.

In the electrical manufacturing study, similar results were obtained. Thus the greater the external orientation, the faster the response time.

Once again, some descriptive data helped us round out the portrait of the responding firms. In particular, the mechanism through which the responding firms learned of the action or move was critical: The most important mechanism in terms of frequency was through customers (44%), followed by advertising or marketing (22%). However, the response lag was shortest when the mechanism was a competitor announcement (1 month) or use of its own sales force (5 months). Also, the goal of the responding firm was critical: As one might expect, the response lag was longest (13.62 months) when the goal was overall profit improvement.

Chapter 6 examined the dynamics of the competitive environments of three different industry types: emerging growth (the electrical-manufacturing study and the high-tech study), fragmented (computer retailing), and mature (the airlines). There were dramatic differences in the percentage of strategic actions taken, as well as the actual number of days it took to evoke both strategic and tactical responses, across these three industrial settings. Also, firms were less likely to imitate actions in the emerging growth industry than in the mature and fragmented industries.

In Chapter 7 there was an analysis of the relationship between move timing and organizational performance. Such an analysis logically follows from the emphasis on response as a dependent variable in the previous chapters, as it is also important to ascertain when response is related to organizational performance. Given the vast but mixed literature on the first mover effect, which has shown that sometimes the first firm to take an action gains a major competitive advantage that is sometimes subsequently lost to a firm using a fast second strategy that avoids the mistakes made by the first-moving firm, we included the initial move and all of the responses to it in this examination of the airline data. There was a significant correlation between response timing and order, and the use of both of these measures suggests that a slow second strategy for easy-to-imitate moves is preferable to being a first mover, a fast second, a slow third, and a late mover.

Chapter 8 focused on why and when firms would cooperate rather than compete with one another. Overall, the analysis of trends suggests that such cooperation does result in higher profits for the cooperating firms. These findings tend to support the rich theory from economics, anecdotal evidence, and the few studies that have actually attempted to test the relationship between cooperation and profits. Thus, while most of our research has concentrated on the dynamics of competitive strategy and the competitive nature of firms in an industry, this chapter suggests that firms should frequently want to cooperate with one another, and with good reason, as profits of all supposed competitors can be enhanced.

Although there is strong confirmation of the model in this research, as described above, there were some independent variables that had either an inconsistent relationship with the response measures or one that was in the opposite direction to that predicted. These included the scope of the action (affecting few to many competitors), a firm's history of past actions, and absorbed and unabsorbed slack. Such results may have occurred for several reasons, including the inadequacy of our communication-information model to include all of the major aspects of competitive dynamics, the possibility that the variables themselves require redefinition, and measurement errors. As suggested in the chapters themselves, there are some possible explanations for these findings, but they clearly are not explicable, given our data bases. Additional research on these issues is strongly suggested.

In summary, our research from four studies, within three different industries, offers clear support for the communication-information model of competitive dynamics, although it does not preclude the use of supplementary or alternative approaches such as game theory. There was clear confirmation of the model and its four components as they relate to predicting different competitive responses, and our findings were consistently in line with the predictions that were derived from the model itself. We recognize the need for a good amount of additional research, and we have included a separate section in each of the substantive chapters that directly addresses this issue. Still, the results lead us to conclude this book with the belief that competitive dynamics can be effectively studied through the use of the communication-information model and the new measurement techniques that we have devised.

References

Adams, J. S. (1976). The structure and dynamics of behavior in organization boundary roles. In M. D. Dunnette (Ed.), *Handbook of industrial and organizational psychology* (pp. 1175-1198). Chicago: Rand McNally.

Air Carrrier Financial Statistics. (various). Washington, DC: U.S. Department of Transportation.

Aldrich, H. E. (1979). *Organizations and environments.* Englewood Cliffs, NJ: Prentice-Hall.

Allison, G. T. (1971). *Essence of decision: Explaining the Cuban missile crisis.* Boston: Little, Brown.

Andrews, K. (1980). *The concept of corporate strategy* (2nd ed.). Homewood, IL: Irwin.

Asch, P., & Seneca, J. (1975, March). Characteristics of collusive firms. *Journal of Industrial Economics*, 223-236.

Bain, J. S. (1956). *Barriers to new competition.* Cambridge, MA: Harvard University Press

Bain, J. S. (1960). Price leaders, barometers, and kinks. *Journal of Business, 33,* 193-203.

Baldwin, W. L., & Childs, G. L. (1969). The fast second and rivalry in research and development. *Southern Economic Journal, 36,* 18-24.

Barnard, C. I. (1938). The functions of the executive. Cambridge, MA: Harvard University Press.

Barney, J. B. (1986). Types of competition and the theory of strategy: Toward an integrative framework. *Academy of Management Review, 11*, 791-800.

Baumol, W. (1972). *Economic theory and operations analysis*. Englewood Cliffs, NJ: Prentice-Hall.

Bedeian, A. G. (1984). *Organizations: Theory and analysis* (rev. ed.). Hinsdale, IL: Dryden Press.

Berlo, D. K. (1960). *The process of communication*. New York: Holt.

Bettis, R. A., & Weeks, D. (1987). Financial returns and strategic interaction: The case of instant photography. *Strategic Management Journal, 8*, 549-563.

Bishop, R. L. (1960). Duopoly: Collusion or warfare? *American Economic Review, 50*, 933-961.

Bond, R., & Lean, D. (1979, October). *Consumer preference, advertising, and sales: On the advantage from early entry* (Federal Trade Commission Bureau of Economics Working Paper No. 14).

Boston Consulting Group, The. (1974). *Perspectives on experience*. Boston: Author.

Bouchard, T. J., Jr. (1976). Unobtrusive measures: An inventory of uses. *Sociological Methods and Research, 4*, 267-300.

Boulding, W., & Moore, M. J. (1987). *Pioneering and profitability: Structural estimates from a nonlinear simultaneous equation model with endogenous pioneering*. Research paper, Fuqua School of Business, Duke University.

Bourgeois, L. J. (1981). On the measurement of organizational slack. *Academy of Management Review, 6*, 29-39.

Bowman, E. H. (1980). A risk/return paradox for strategic management. *Sloan Management Review, 21*, 17-31.

Bowman, E. H. (1982). Risk seeking by troubled firms. *Sloan Management Review, 23*, 33-42.

Brenner, M. H., & Sigband, N. B. (1973). Organizational communication-analysis based on empirical data. *Academy of Management Journal, 16*, 323-324.

Buzzell, R. D., & Ferris, P. (1977). Marketing costs in consumer goods industries. In H. Thorelli (Ed.), *Strategy + structure = performance* (pp. 122-145). Bloomington: Indiana University Press.

Buzzell, R. D., Gale, B. T., & Sultan, R. G. (1975, January-February). Market share—A key to profitability. *Harvard Business Review*, 97-106.

Campbell, D. T., & Fiske, D. W. (1959). Convergent and discriminant validation by the multitrait-multimethod matrix. *Psychological Bulletin, 56*, 81-105.

Carson, R. O. (1972). *School superintendents: Career and performance*. Columbus, OH: Merrill.

Caves, R. E. (1984, May). Economic analysis and the quest for competitive advantage. *Papers and Proceedings of the 96th Annual Meeting of the American Economic Association*, 127-132.

Caves, R. E., & Porter, M. E. (1977). From entry barriers to mobility barriers: Conjectural decisions and contrived deterrence to new competition. *Quarterly Journal of Economics, 91*, 241-262.

Chakravarthy, B. S. (1982). Adaptation: A promising metaphor for strategic management. *Academy of Management Review, 7*, 35-44.

Chamberlain, E. (1957). *The theory of monopolistic competition*. Cambridge, MA: Harvard University Press.

Chen, M. J. (1988). *Competitive strategic interaction: A study of competitive actions and responses*. Doctoral dissertation, University of Maryland at College Park.

Child, J. (1974). Managerial and organizational factors associated with company performance. *Journal of Management Studies, 11*, 13-27.

Cohen, A. R. (1958). Upward communication in experimentally created hierarchies. *Human Relations, 18*, 41-53.

Conrath, D. W. (1967). Organizational decision making behavior under varying conditions of uncertainty. *Management Science, 13*, 487-500.

Cool, K. O., & Schendel, D. E. (1987). Strategic group formation and performance: U.S. pharmaceutical industry. *Management Science, 33*, 1102-1124.

Cooper, A. C., & Schendel, D. (1976). Strategic responses to technological threats. *Business Horizons, 19*, 61-69.

Cyert, R. M., & March, J. G. (1963). *A behavioral theory of the firm*. Englewood Cliffs, NJ: Prentice-Hall.

Daft, R. L., & Lengel, R. H. (1984). Information richness: A new approach to managerial behavior and organization design. *Research in Organizational Behavior, 6*, 191-233.

Denzin, N. K. (1978). *The research act*. New York: McGraw-Hill.

Dess, G. G., & Beard, D. W. (1984). Dimensions of organizational task environments. *Administrative Science Quarterly, 17*, 313-327.

Dess, G. G., & Davis, P. S. 1984). Porter's generic strategies as determinants of strategic group membership and organizational performance. *Academy of Management Journal, 27*, 467-488.

Diamond, D. W. (1984). Financial intermediation and delegated monitoring. *Review of Economic Studies, LI*, 393-414.

Downs, A. (1966). *Inside bureaucracy*. Boston: Little, Brown.

Dun and Bradstreet Corporate Directory. (various). Parsippany, NJ: Dun's Marketing Service.

Duncan, R. B. (1972). Characteristics of organizational environments and perceived environmental uncertainty. *Administrative Science Quarterly, 17*, 313-327.

Duncan, R. B. (1973). Multiple decision-making structures in adapting to environmental uncertainty: The impact of organizational effectiveness. *Human Relations, 26*, 273-291.

Dutton, J. E., & Jackson, S. B. (1987). Categorizing strategic issues: Links to organizational action. *Academy of Management Review, 12*, 76-90.

Eaton, B. C., & Lipsey, R. G. (1981). Capital, commitment, and entry equilibrium. *Bell Journal of Economics, 12*, 593-604.

Eaton, B. C., & Ware, R. (1987). A theory of market structure with sequential entry. *Rand Journal of Economics, 18*, 1-16.

Egelhoff, W. G. (1982). Strategy and structure in multinational corporations: An information-processing approach. *Administrative Science Quarterly, 17*, 313-327.

Emery, F. E., & Trist, E. L. (1965). The causal texture of organizational environments. *Human Relations, 18*, 21-32.

Farrell, J. & Saloner, G. (1986). Installed base and compatibility: Innovation, product preannouncements and predation. *American Economic Review, 76*, 940-955.

Fellner, W. (1949). *Competition among the few*. New York: Knopf.

Fisher, B. A. (1978). *Perspectives on human communication*. New York: Macmillan.

Fombrun, C., & Shanley, M. (1990). What's in a name? Reputation building and corporate strategy. *Academy of Management Journal, 33*, 233-258.

Fraas, A. G., & Greer, D. (1977). Market structure and price collusion: An empirical analysis. *Journal of Industrial Economics, 26*, 21-43.

Fudenberg, D., Gilbert, R., Stiglitz, J., & Tirole, J. (1983). Preemption, leapfrogging, and competition in patent races. *European Economic Review, 22*, 3-31.

Gal-Or, E. (1985). First mover and second mover advantages. *International Economic Review, 26*, 649-653.

Galbraith, J. R. (1973). *Designing complex organizations*. Reading, MA: Addison-Wesley.

Galbraith, J. R. (1977). *Organization design*. Reading, MA: Addison-Wesley.

Glazer, A. (1985). The advantages of being first. *American Economic Review, 75*, 473-480.

Glick, W. H., & Roberts, K. H. (1984). Hypothesized interdependence, assumed independence. *Academy of Management Review, 9*, 722-735.

Gollop, F., & Roberts, M. (1979). Firm interdependence in oligopolistic markets. *Journal of Econometrics, 10*, 313-331.

Gort, M., & Klepper, S. (1982). Time paths in the diffusion of product innovations. *Economic Journal, 92*, 640-642.

Greenhalgh, L. (1983). Organizational decline. In S. Bacharach (Ed.), *Research in the sociology of organizations* (pp. 231-276). Greenwich, CT: JAI Press.

Guetzkow, H. (1965). Communications in organization. In J. March (Ed.), *Handbook of organizations* (pp. 534-573). Chicago: Rand McNally.

Hambrick, D. C. (1983). High profit strategies in mature capital goods industries: A contingency approach. *Academy of Management Journal, 26*(4), 687-707.

Hambrick, D. C., & Mason, P. A. (1984). Upper echelons: The organization as a reflection of its top managers. *Academy of Management Review, 9*(2), 193-206.

Hannan, M., & Freeman, J. (1977). The population ecology of organizations. *American Journal of Sociology, 83*, 929-964.

Harrigan, K. R. (1980). The effect of exit barriers upon strategic flexibility. *Strategic Management Journal, 1*, 165-176.

Harrigan, K. R. (1982). Exit decisions in mature industries. *Academy of Management Journal, 25*(4), 707-732.

Harrigan, K. R. (1983). Research methodologies for contingency approaches to business strategy. *Academy of Management Review, 8*, 398-405.

Harrigan, K. R. (1985). *Strategic flexibility: A management guide for changing times*. Lexington, MA: Lexington Books.

Hatten, K. T., Schendel, D. E., & Cooper, A. C. (1978). A strategic model of the U.S. brewing industry: 1952-1971. *Academy of Management Journal, 21*, 592-610.

Hayes, R. H., & Abernathy, W. J. (1980, July-August). Managing our way to economic decline. *Harvard Business Review*, 67-77.

Hewes, D. I., Graham, M. L., Doelger, J., & Pavitt, C. (1985). Second guessing: Message interpretation in social networks. *Human Communication Research, 11*, 299-334.

Hinnings, C. R., Hickson, D. J., Pennings, J. M., & Schneck, R. E. (1974). Structural conditions of intraorganizational power. *Administrative Science Quarterly, 19*, 22-44.

Hirschman, A. O. (1964). The paternity of an index. *American Economic Review, 54*, 761-765.

Hitt, M. A., & Barr, S. H. (1989). Managerial selection decision models: Examination of configural cue processing. *Journal of Applied Psychology, 74*, 53-61.

Huber, G. P. (1982). Organizational information systems: Determinants of their performances and behavior. *Management Science, 32*, 572-589.

Huber, G. P., & Daft, R. L. (1987). The information environments of organizations. In F. M. Jablin, L. L. Putnam, K. H. Roberts, & L. Porter (Eds.), *Handbook of organizational communication* (pp. 130-164). Newbury Park, CA: Sage.

Huber, G. P., & Power, D. J. (1984). Retrospective reports of strategic-level managers: Guidelines for increasing their accuracy. *Strategic Management Journal, 6*, 171-180.

Huber, G. P., & Ullman, J. C. (1973). *The local job bank program.* Lexington, MA: D. C. Heath.

Jablin, F. M. (1987). Formal organizational structure. In F. M. Jablin, L. L. Putnam, K. H. Roberts, & L. Porter (Eds.), *Handbook of organizational communication* (pp. 389-419). Newbury Park, CA: Sage.

Jablin, F. M., Putnam, L. L., Roberts, K. H., & Porter, L. (Eds.). (1987). *Handbook of organizational communication.* Newbury Park, CA: Sage.

Jauch, L. R., Osborn, R. N., & Martin, T. N. (1980). Structured content analysis of cases: A complementary method for organizational research. *Academy of Management Review, 5*, 517-526.

Jensen, M., & Meckling, W. (1976). Theory of the firm: Managerial behavior, agency costs, and ownership structure. *Journal of Financial Economics, 3*, 305-360.

Jick, T. O. (1979). Mixing qualitative and quantitative methods: Triangulation in action. *Administrative Science Quarterly, 24*, 602-611.

Joskow, P. (1975). Firm decision making processes and oligopoly theory. *American Economic Review, LXV*, 270-279.

Jurkovich, R. (1974). A core typology of organizational environments. *Administrative Science Quarterly, 19*, 380-394.

Kamien, M. I., & Schwartz, N. L. (1978). Potential rivalry, monopoly profits and the pace of inventive activity. *Review of Economic Studies, 45*, 547-557.

Karnani, A., & Wernerfelt, B. (1985). Multiple point competition. *Strategic Management Journal, 6*, 87-96.

Katz, M. L., & Shapiro, C. (1987). R&D rivalry with licensing or imitation. *American Economic Review, 77*, 402-420.

Knight, K. E., & McDaniel, R. R. (1979). *Organizations: An information systems perspective.* Belmont, CA: Wadsworth.

Kreps, D. M. (1990). *Game theory and economic modeling.* Oxford, UK: Oxford University Press.

Kreps, D. M., & Wilson, R. (1982a). Sequential equilibria. *Econometrica, 4*, 863-894.

Kreps, D. M., & Wilson, R. (1982b). Reputation and imperfect information. *Journal of Economic Theory, 27*, 253-279.

Kwoka, J., & Ravenscraft, D. (1986). Cooperation v. rivalry: Price-cost margins by line of business. *Economica, 53*, 351-363.

Lawrence, P. R., & Lorsch, J. W. (1967). *Organization and environment.* Homewood, IL: Irwin.

Lazarsfeld, P. F., & Merton, R. K. (1964). Friendship as social process: A substantive and methodological analysis. In M. Berger (Ed.), *Freedom and control in modern society* (pp. 18-66). New York: Octagon.

Levin, R., Klevorick, A., Nelson, R., & Winter, S. (1987). *Appropriating the returns from industrial research and development* (Brookings Papers on Economic Activity, No. 3).

Lieberman, M. B., & Montgomery, D. B. (1988). First-mover advantages. *Strategic Management Journal, 9*, 41-58.

Lindblom, C. E. (1959). The science of muddling through. *Public Administration Review, 19*, 79-88.

Locke, E. A., & Latham, G. P. (1990). *A theory of goal setting & task performance.* Englewood Cliffs, NJ: Prentice-Hall.

Lubatkin, M. H., Chung, K. H., Rogers, R. C., & Owers, J. E. (1989). Stockholder reaction to CEO changes in large corporations. *Academy of Management Journal, 6*, 75-86.

MacMillan, I. (1983). Preemptive strategies. *Journal of Business Strategy, 4*(2), 16-26.

MacMillan, I., McCaffrey, M. L., & Van Wijk, G. (1985). Competitor's responses to easily imitated new products: Exploring commercial banking product introductions. *Strategic Management Journal, 6*, 75-86.

MacMillan, I. C. (1988). Controlling competitive dynamics by taking strategic initiative. *The Academy of Management Executives, II*(2), 111-118.

Maddala, G. S. (1977). *Econometrics*. New York: McGraw-Hill.

Mann, H. M. (1966, August). Seller concentration, barriers to entry, and rates of return in thirty industries, 1950-1960. *Review of Economics and Statistics, 48*, 296-307.

Mansfield, E. (1985). How rapidly does new technology leak out? *Journal of Industrial Economics, 34*(2), 217-233.

Mansfield, E., Schwartz, M., & Wagner, S. (1981). Imitation costs and patents: An empirical study. *Economic Journal, 91*, 907-918.

March, J. G., & Simon, H. A. (1958). *Organizations*. New York: John Wiley.

Markham, J. (1951). The nature and significance of price leadership. *American Economic Review, 41*, 891-905.

Mason, E. (1939, March). Price and production policies of large-scale enterprise. *American Economic Review*, 61-74.

McGrath J. E. (1964). Toward a "theory of method" for research on organizations. In W. W. Cooper H. L. Leavitt, & M. W. Shelly (Eds.), *New perspectives in organizational research* (pp. 533-547). Summerset, NJ: John Wiley.

McPhee, R. D., & Tompkin, P. K. (1985). *Organizational communication: Traditional themes and new directions*. Beverly Hills, CA: Sage.

Meyer, A. D. (1982). Adapting to environmental jolts. *Administrative Science Quarterly, 27*, 515-537.

Miles, R. E., & Snow, C. C. (1978). *Organizational strategy, structure, and process.* New York: McGraw-Hill.

Miles, R. H. (1980). *Macro organizational behavior*. Santa Monica, CA: Goodyear.

Milgrom, P., & Roberts, J. (1982). Predation, reputation, and entry deterrence. *Journal of Economic Theory, 27*, 280-312.

Miller, D., & Friesen, P. (1978). Archetypes of strategy formulation. *Management Science, 24*, 221-236.

Miller, D., & Friesen, P. H. (1984). *Organizations: A quantum view.* Englewood Cliffs, NJ: Prentice-Hall.

Miller, J. G. (1972). Living systems: The organization. *Behavioral Science, 17*, 182.

Mintzberg, H. (1973). Patterns in strategy formation. *Management Science, 24*, 934-938.

Mintzberg, H. (1978). Patterns of strategy formation. *Management Science, 24* 934-948.

Mortensen, D. C. (1972). *Communication.* New York: McGraw-Hill.

Nash, J. (1950). Equilibrium points in n-person games. *Proceedings of the National Academy of Sciences, Washington, D.C.*

Nelson, R. R., & Winter, S. G. (1982). *An evolutionary theory of economic change.* Cambridge, MA: Harvard University Press.

Nomani, A. Q. (1991, June 21). NWA, TWA agree to alter pricing actions. *Wall Street Journal*, p. B1.

Oliva, T. A., Day, D. L., & MacMillan, I. C., (1988). A generic model of competitive dynamics. *Academy of Management Review, 13*(3), 374-389.

O'Reilly, C. A., & Roberts, K. (1974). Information filtration in organizations: Three experiments. *Organizational Behavior and Human Performance, 11*, 153-265.

Osborne, D. K. (1976). Cartel problems. *American Economic Review, 66*, 835-844.

Osborne, M., & Pitchik, O. (1983). Profit-sharing in a collusive industry. *European Economic Review, 22*, 59-74.

Oster, S. M. (1990). *Modern competitive analysis.* New York: Oxford University Press.

Pearce, J. A., II. (1983). The relationship of internal versus external orientations to financial measures of strategic performance. *Strategic Management Journal, 4*, 297-306.

Pennings, J. M. (1975). The relevance of the structural-contingency model of organizational effectiveness. *Administrative Science Quarterly, 20*, 393-410.

Peters, T., & Waterman, R. (1982). *In search of excellence.* New York: Harper & Row.

Pfeffer, J. (1972). Size and composition of corporate boards of directors: The organization and its environment. *Administrative Science Quarterly, 2*, 218-228.

Pindyck, R. S., & Rubinfeld, D. L. (1981). *Econometric models and economic forecasts.* New York: McGraw-Hill.

Porac, J. F., & Thomas, H. (1990). Taxonomic mental models in competitor definition. *Academy of Management Review, 15*, 224-240.

Porter, M. E. (1979). The structure within industries and companies performance. *Review of Economics and Statistics, 61*, 214-227.

Porter, M. E. (1980). *Competitive strategy: Techniques for analyzing industries and competitors.* New York: Free Press.

Porter, M. E. (1984). Strategic interaction: Some lessons from industry histories for theory and antitrust policy. In R. B. Lamb (Ed.), *Competitive strategic management* (pp. 415-445). Englewood Cliffs, NJ: Prentice-Hall.

Porter, M. E. (1985). *Competitive advantage: Creating and sustaining superior performance.* New York: Free Press.

Porter, M. E. (1990). *The competitive advantage of nations.* New York: Free Press.

Porter, R. (1983). A study of cartel stability: The joint executive committee: 1880-1886. *Bell Journal of Economics 14*(2), 301-314.

Prescott, J. E., Kohli, A. K., & Venkatramen, N. (1986). The market share-profitability relationship: An empirical assessment of major assertions and contradictions. *Strategic Management Journal, 7,* 377-394.

Rapoport, A. (1966). *Two-person game theory.* Ann Arbor: University of Michigan Press.

Reich, R. B. (1983, April). The next American frontier. *The Atlantic Monthly,* pp. 97-108.

Reynolds, L. G. (1940). Cutthroat competition. *American Economic Review, 30,* 736-747.

Robinson, W. T. (1988, February). Sources of market pioneer advantages: The case of industrial goods industries. *Journal of Marketing Research,* 87-94.

Robinson, W. T., & Fornell, C. (1985). The sources of market pioneer advantages in consumer goods industries. *Journal of Marketing Research, 22,* 305-317.

Rogers, E. M. (1983). *The diffusion of innovation.* New York: Free Press.

Rogers, E. M., & Shoemaker, F. F. (1971). *Communication of innovations.* New York: Free Press.

Rotemberg, J., & Saloner, G. (1985, September). *Price leadership* (MIT Department of Economics Working Paper No. 388).

Rousseau, D. M. (1978). Characteristics of departments, positions and individuals: Context for attitudes and behaviors. *Administrative Science Quarterly, 23,* 521-540.

Scherer, F. M. (1967, August). Research and development resource allocation under rivalry. *Quarterly Journal of Economics,* 359-394.

Scherer, F. M., & Ross, D. (1990). *Industrial market structure and economic performance.* Boston: Houghton Mifflin.

Schmalensee, R. (1972). *The economics of advertising.* Amsterdam: North-Holland.

Schnaars, S. P. (1986, March-April). When entering growth markets, are pioneers better than poachers? *Business Horizons,* 27-36.

Schumpeter, J. A. (1934). *The theory of economic development.* Cambridge, MA: Harvard University Press.

Schumpeter, J. A. (1950). *Capitalism, socialism, and democracy* (3rd. ed.). New York: Harper.

Shannon, C., & Weaver, W. (1949). *The mathematical theory of communication.* Urbana: University of Illinois Press.

Shapiro, C. (1983). Premiums for high quality products as returns to reputations. *Quarterly Journal of Economics, 98,* 659-679.

Shaw, R. W., & Shaw, S. A. (1984). Late entry market shares, and competitive survival: The case of synthetic fibers. *Managerial and Decision Economics, 5,* 72-79.

Simon, H. A. (1973). Applying information technology to organization design. *Public Administration Review, 33,* 268-278.

Simon, H. A. (1979). *Marketing multiplier and marketing strategy: Simplified dynamic decision rules* (Working paper, 1050-79, Massachussetts Institute of Technology).

Simon, H. A. (1980). PRICESTRAT-An applied strategic pricing model for non-durables. In A. Zoltners (Ed.), *Marketing planning models, TIMS studies in the management sciences.* New York: North-Holland.

Singh, J. V. (1986). Performance, slack, and risk taking in organizational decision making. *Academy of Management Journal, 29,* 562-585.

Smith, K. G., & Grimm, C. M. (1987). *Gambit and repartee: A theory of competitive action and response.* Presented at the Academy of Management, Business Policy and Planning Division, New Orleans, Louisiana.

Smith, K. G., & Grimm, C. M. (1991). A communication/information processing model of competitive response timing. *Journal of Management, 17*(1), 5-23.

Smith, K. G., Grimm, C. M., Chen, M. J., & Gannon, M. J. (1989). Predictors of competitive strategic actions: Theory and preliminary evidence. *Journal of Business Research, 18,* 245-258.

Smith, K. G., Grimm, C. M., & Gannon, M. J., (1990). Competitive moves and responses among high-technology firms. In H. E. Glass (Ed.), *Handbook of business strategy* (ch. 31, pp. 1-11). Boston: Warren, Gorham & Lamont.

Smith, K. G., Grimm, C. M., Gannon, M. J., & Chen, M. J. (1991). Organizational information-processing, competitive responses and performance in the U.S. domestic airline industry. *Academy of Management Journal, 34*(1), 60-85.

Smith, K. G., Mitchell, T. R., & Summer, C. E. (1985). Top level management priorities in different stages of the organizational life cycle. *Academy of Management Journal, 28*(4), 799-820.

Spence, A. M. (1977). Entry, capacity, investment, and oligopolistic pricing. *Bell Journal of Economics, 8,* 534-544.

Stigler, G. J. (1947). The kinky oligopoly demand curve and rigid prices. *Journal of Political Economy, 55,* 432-449.

Sullivan, L. A. (1977). *Handbook of the law of antitrust.* St. Paul: West.

Taylor, L., & Weiserbs, D. (1972). Advertising and the aggregate consumption function. *American Economic Review, 62,* 642-655.

Teece, D. J. (1986). Profiting from technological innovation: Implications for integration, collaboration, licensing and public policy. *Research Policy, 15,* 285-305.

Thompson, J. (1967). *Organizations in action.* New York: McGraw-Hill.

Tirole, J. (1989). *The theory of industrial organization.* Cambridge: MIT Press.

Tushman, M. L., & Nadler, D. A. (1978). Information processing as an integrating concept in organizational design. *Academy of Management Review, 3,* 613-624.

Van de Ven, A. H., Delbecq, A. L., & Koenig, R. (1976). Determinants of coordination modes within organizations. *American Sociological Review, 41,* 322-338.

Von Neumann, J., & Morgenstern, O. (1944). *Theory of games and economic behavior.* Princeton: Princeton University Press.

Weigelt, K., & Camerer, C. (1988). Reputation and corporate strategy: A review of rent theory and applications. *Strategic Management Journal, 9,* 443-454,

Weigelt, K., & MacMillan, I. (1988). An interactive strategic analysis framework. *Strategic Management Journal, 9,* 27-40.

Wernerfelt, B., & Karnani, A. (1987). Competitive strategy under uncertainty. *Strategic Management Journal, 8,* 187-194.

Williamson, O. E. (1965). A dynamic theory of interfirm behavior. *Quarterly Journal of Economics, 79*, 579-607.

Williamson, O. E. (1985). *The economic institutions of capitalism*. New York: Free Press.

Wilson, R. (1985). Reputation in games and markets. In A. E. Roth (Ed.), *Game-theoretic models of bargaining* (pp. 27-62). Cambridge, UK: Cambridge University Press.

Wissema, J. G., Van der Pol, H. W., & Messer, H. M. (1980). Strategic management archetypes. *Strategic Management Journal, 1*(1), 37-47.

World Aviation Directory. (various). Washington, DC: American Aviation Publications, McGraw-Hill.

Yamey, B. S. (1972). Predatory price cutting: Notes and comments. *Journal of Law and Economics, 15*, 137-147.

Yip, G. S. (1982). *Barriers to entry: A corporate-strategy perspective*. Lexington, MA: Lexington Books.

Zeithaml, C. P., & Fry, L. W. (1984). Contextual and strategic differences among mature businesses in four dynamic performance situations. *Academy of Management Journal, 27*(4), 841-860.

Zey-Ferrell, M. (1979). *Dimensions of organizations: Environment, context, structure, process and performance*. Santa Monica, CA: Goodyear.

Zucker, A. (1965). On the desirability of price instability. *Econometrica, 33*, 437-441.

Author Index

Subject Index

About the Authors

Martin J. Gannon received his Ph.D. from the Graduate School of Business, Columbia University. Currently Professor of Management, College of Business and Management, University of Maryland at College Park, he has also served within this college as Acting Associate Dean for Academic Affairs, Chairperson of the Faculty of Management and Organizational Behavior, and Co-Director of the Small Business Development Center. A former senior Research Fulbright Professor, University of Kassel, West Germany, and the John F. Kennedy/Fulbright Professor of Management of Thammasat University, Bangkok, Thailand, Dr. Gannon is a past president and fellow, Eastern Academy of Management, and past chairperson of the Human Resources Division of the Academy of Management. He has served as a management trainer and consultant to a number of private firms and government agencies and has authored or co-authored 75 papers and articles, in addition to writing *Management: Managing for Results, Organizational Behavior, Management: An Integrated Framework*, and co-editing *Readings in Management*. He is currently working on a book tentatively titled *Cultural Metaphors*.

Curtis M. Grimm is Associate Professor of Transportation, Business, and Public Policy, College of Business and Management, University of Maryland at College Park. He has been a member of this college since 1983. He received his B.A. in economics from the University of Wisconsin-Madison and his Ph.D. in economics from the University of California-Berkeley, where doctoral course work included a concentration in industrial organization. His research, which involves the interface of public policy and strategic management, with a particular focus on transportation, has resulted in more than 35 publications in leading strategic management and transportation journals, including *Academy of Management Journal, Management Science, Strategic Management Journal, Journal of Management, Transportation Research, Transportation Journal*, and *Logistics and Transportation Review*. He recently co-authored *The Economic Effects of Surface Freight Deregulation*. In addition to serving as an economic consultant for such government agencies as the Interstate Commerce Commission, the Postal Rate Commission, the General Accounting Office, the Maryland Department of Employment and Economic Development, and the Canadian Department of Consumer and Corporate Affairs, he has consulted for the National Industrial Transportation League and the Grand Trunk Western Railroad.

Ken G. Smith is Professor of Strategic Management in the College of Business and Management at the University of Maryland at College Park. He received his M.B.A. in organizational behavior from the University of Rhode Island in 1972; and his Ph.D. from the University of Washington in Seattle in 1983, following 8 years as an entrepreneur and chief executive officer in the pump and marine products industries. He has published more than 40 articles in journals such as *Academy of Management Journal, Strategic Management Journal, Management Science,* and *Organizational Behavior and Human Decision Processes.* In addition, he has presented numerous papers at national and international meetings, and at many different universities. He is a leader in the field of strategic management, where his research on the relationship between strategy and organizational performance is well known. His research has been supported by University of Maryland General Research Grants and Scholastic Achievement Awards and by the Small Business Administration. Dr. Smith is on the editorial review boards of the *Academy of Management Journal, Academy of Management Executive,* and the *Journal of Management.* He was awarded the IBM/Alan Krowe Teaching Award for teaching excellence in 1987 and 1990. Dr. Smith is Co-Director of Research and Director of Academic Programs for the Michael D. Dingman Entrepreneurship Center and has been a consultant to a variety of organizations.